KAPPIYA'S STORY COLLECTIONS 8

ZEN STORIES

KAPPIYA CLASSICS

Contents

Foreword

KAPPIYA CLASSICS

Hello Dear Readers

I am Tamizhiniya Tamizhdesan

when I was studying in school my teachers used to conduct lessons between many good books and that conduct gave me confidence that I can conduct more than a hundred topics with introductory speech. My Technical education helped a lot in this aspect. When I became a teacher I assisted my students in the way our teachers guided us.

My school, college and workplace friends lives scattered in different countries like the poem of Eelam Poet V.I.S. Jayapalan, the families of them too scattered in different nation, whereas I live in the Land of my Mother Language(Tamilnadu). Among my friends who are running to strive for their living, I have selected the publishing department to read their lives and pass it on to others. We are publishing legendary works under Kappiya Vasipagam. So far we have published more than 1500 books in package type.

I have used the library a lot in my school, college and work life. Novelist Vasu Murugavel writes that he brought a bundle of books from a person, read them and returned them. Similarly, I have imported hundreds of books read them and sent them back. I have also written novel in Tamil and English, also a book based on the Culture of Tamil People.

My son Imayakappiyan (8) started learning his Tamil lettering from the texts of our cover pages. The same way he is gaining the knowledge of book names, authors also the technical knowledge in publishing and helps us in many ways. My husband Tamizhdesan guides me about the packaging materials of the book contents and his creative thinking of book cover page makes me to create some unique cover pages. We three feel very happy to be in this field which makes us to learn continuously.

I take great pleasure in publishing many of the war stories I have been reading. Movements that fight for the people are viewed by populists as scumbags. An example of this is the Tiger movement, which was not only similar to a government but also created various departments and the personality within them. There is no doubt that writing and reading them as well will diversify you.

CHAPTER ONE

ZEN STORIES

Zen is a school of *Mahāyāna* ("Larger Vehicle") Buddhism that is most famous in Japan. The word Zen is from the Japanese pronunciation of the Chinese word Chán (禪), which in turn is derived from the Sanskrit word dhyāna, which can be approximately translated as "meditation" or "meditative state"

Zen emphasizes experiential wisdom in the attainment of enlightenment. As such, it de-emphasizes theoretical knowledge in favor of direct self-realization through meditation and dharma practice. The teachings of Zen include various sources of Mahāyāna thought, including the Prajñāpāramitā literature and the teachings of the Yogācāra and Tathāgatagarbha schools

The philosophy of Zen and the practice which go with it aim at enlarging our awareness. This is to say awareness of ourselves and our environment. Zen is an exercise in self knowledge in which concentration is the most important method.

1. *Learning the Hard Way*

The son of a master thief asked his father to teach him the secrets of the trade.

The old thief agreed and that night took his son to burglarize a large house.

While the family was asleep, he silently led his young apprentice into a room that contained a clothes closet. The father told his son to go into the closet to pick out some clothes. When he did, his father quickly shut the door and locked him in.

Then he went back outside, knocked loudly on the front door, thereby waking the family, and quickly slipped away before anyone saw him.

Hours later, his son returned home, bedraggled and exhausted.

"Father," he cried angrily, "Why did you lock me in that closet? If I hadn't been made desperate by my fear of getting caught, I never would have escaped. It took all my ingenuity to get out!"

The old thief smiled. "Son, you have had your first lesson in the art of burglary."

Reflection: A challenge always brings out the most in a man. Your mind works best and faster when you have your back to the wall.

2. _More is not Enough_

There was once a stone cutter who was dissatisfied with himself and with his position in life.

One day he passed a wealthy merchant's house. Through the open gateway, he saw many fine possessions and important visitors. "How powerful that merchant must be!" thought the stone cutter. He became very envious and wished that he could be like the merchant.

To his great surprise, he suddenly became the merchant, enjoying more luxuries and power than he had ever imagined, but envied and detested by those less wealthy than himself. Soon a high official passed by, carried in a sedan chair, accompanied by attendants and escorted by soldiers beating gongs. Everyone, no matter how wealthy, had to bow low before the procession. "How powerful that official is!" he thought. "I wish that I could be a high official!"

Then he became the high official, carried everywhere in his embroidered sedan chair, feared and hated by the people all around. It was a hot summer day, so the official felt very uncomfortable in the sticky sedan chair. He looked up at the sun. It shone proudly in the sky, unaffected by his presence. "How powerful the sun is!" he thought. "I wish that I could be the sun!"

Then he became the sun, shining fiercely down on everyone, scorching the fields, cursed by the farmers and laborers. But a huge black cloud moved between him and the earth, so that his light could no longer shine on everything below. "How powerful that storm cloud is!" he thought. "I wish that I could be a cloud!"

Then he became the cloud, flooding the fields and villages, shouted at by everyone. But soon he found that he was being pushed away by some great force, and realized that it was the wind. "How powerful it is!" he thought. "I wish that I could be the wind!"

Then he became the wind, blowing tiles off the roofs of houses, uprooting trees, feared and hated by all below him. But after a while, he ran up against something that would not move, no matter how forcefully he blew against it - a huge, towering rock. "How powerful that rock is!" he thought. "I wish that I could be a rock!"

Then he became the rock, more powerful than anything else on earth. But as he stood there, he heard the sound of a hammer pounding a chisel into the hard surface, and felt himself being changed. "What could be more powerful than I, the rock?" he thought.

He looked down and saw far below him the figure of a stone cutter.

Reflection: The grass is always green on the other side – until you get there. It's a matter of perspective. Satisfaction is a personal choice. Choose to green up your own grass rather than hopping that fence.

3. _Anger_

There was a little boy with a bad temper.

The master told him to hammer a nail in the back fence every time he lost his temper. The first day, the boy drove 37 nails to the fence. He discovered it was easier to hold his temper than to drive those nails into the fence. Finally, the day came when the boy didn't lose his temper at all.

Now the master suggested that the boy pull out one nail for each day that he was able to hold his temper. A few days passed and the young boy finally told the master that all the nails were gone.

The master said, "You have done well my boy, but look at the holes in the fence. The fence will never be the same again."

Reflection - Anger is the most uncultured and uncivilized way of responding to a situation. Burn anger before anger burns you.

4. *Happiness and Prosperity*

A rich man asked a Zen master to write something that the family could cherish for generations.

On a large piece of paper, the master wrote, "Father dies, son dies, grandson dies." The rich man became angry when he saw the master's words.

" If your son should die before you," the master answered, "this would bring unbearable grief to your family. If your grandson should die before your son this would also bring great sorrow. If your family, generations after generation, disappears in the order I have mentioned, it will be the natural course of life. This is true happiness and prosperity."

Reflection: Knowledge has its ways which ignorance knows not. Ask questions to the master; don't question the master.

5. *Chasing Two Rabbits*

A martial arts student approached his teacher with a question. "I'd like to improve my knowledge of the martial arts. So in addition to learning from you, I'd like to study under another teacher in order to learn another style. What do you think of this idea?"

" The hunter who chases two rabbits," answered the master, "catches neither."

Reflection: To excel, one has to focus all energy at the task at hand. Stay focused on one thing. Trying to get everything will get you nothing. Focus is not only your ability to stay attracted to the 'One', but also the discipline to avoid the distraction of the other 'Ninety-nine'

6. *The Nature of Things*

Two monks were washing their bowls in the river when they noticed a scorpion that was drowning.

One monk immediately scooped it up and set it upon the bank. In the process he was stung by the scorpion.

He went back to washing his bowl and again the scorpion fell in. The monk saved the scorpion and was again stung.

The other monk asked him, "Friend, why do you continue to save the scorpion when you know it's nature is to sting?"

"Because," the monk replied, "to sting is the scorpion's nature, but to save it is my nature."

Reflection: Divinity sings from the heart of those who can be good even to those who have not been so good to them.

7. *Working Very Hard*

A martial arts student went to his teacher and said earnestly, "I am devoted to studying your martial arts system. How long will it take me to master it?".

The teacher's reply was casual, "Ten years". Impatiently, the student answered, "But I want to master it faster than that. I will work very hard. I will practice everyday, ten or more hours a day if I have to. How long will it take then?".

The teacher thought for a moment, "20 years", he said.

Reflection: Sometimes, if you try too hard, you just get in your own way. It makes you anxious, which just blocks understanding. Some things have to develop naturally, by themselves. You can't rush true learning. You have to take one step at a time. Mastery doesn't come from practice alone.

8. *Full Awareness*

After ten years of apprenticeship, Tenno achieved the rank of Zen teacher.

One rainy day, he went to visit the famous master Nan-in.

When he walked in, the master greeted him with a question, "Did you leave your wooden clogs and umbrella on the porch?"

"Yes," Tenno replied.

"Tell me," the master continued, "did you place your umbrella to the left of your shoes, or to the right?"

Tenno did not know the answer, and realized that he had not yet attained full awareness.

So he became Nan-in's apprentice and studied under him for ten more years.

Zen principle: Zen is all about the state of being always aware and complete wisdom.

9. *Eating the Blame*

Circumstances arose one day which delayed preparation of the dinner of a Soto Zen master, Fukai, and his followers.

In haste the cook went to the garden with his curved knife and cut off the tops of green vegetables, chopped them together and made soup, unaware that in his haste he had included a part of a snake in the vegetables.

The followers of Fugai thought they never tasted such good soup.

But when the master himself found the snake's head in his bowl, he summoned the cook.

"What is this?" he demanded, holding up the head of the snake.

"Oh, thank you, master," replied the cook, taking the morsel and eating it quickly.

Reflection: Even if you have unintentionally made a mistake, you must at all times be ready to accept the outcome.

10. *The Moon Cannot be Stolen*

Ryokan, a Zen master, lived the simplest kind of life in a little hut at the foot of a mountain. One evening a thief visited the hut only to discover there was nothing in it to steal.

Ryokan returned and caught him. "You may have come a long way to visit me," he told the prowler, "and you should not return empty handed. Please take my clothes as a gift."

The thief was bewildered. He took the clothes and slunk away.

Ryokan sat naked, watching the moon. "Poor fellow, " he mused, "I wish I could give him this beautiful moon."

Reflection: A feeling of lack is one of the most pervasive emotions in our lives. Sometimes we don't even fully recognize it, but immediately run for what we believe will fill our lives, thinking that the next thing on our agenda will make us happy or satisfied.

11. *The Present Moment*

A Japanese warrior was captured by his enemies and thrown into prison. That night he was unable to sleep because he feared that the next day he would be interrogated, tortured and executed. Then, the words of his Zen master came to him. "Tomorrow is not real. It is an illusion. The only reality is now".

Heeding these words, the warrior became peaceful and fell asleep.

Reflection: We always want to plan for the future, but we always make ourselves miserable in the present while doing it.

12. *Useless Life*

A farmer got so old that he couldn't work the fields anymore. So he would spend the day just sitting on the porch.

His son, still working the farm, would look up from time to time and see his father sitting there.

"He's of no use any more," the son thought to himself, "he doesn't do anything!".

One day the son got so frustrated by this, that he built a wood coffin, dragged it over to the porch, and told his father to get in. Without saying anything, the father climbed inside.

After closing the lid, the son dragged the coffin to the edge of the farm where there was a high cliff. As he approached the drop, he heard a light tapping on the lid from inside the coffin.

He opened it up. Still lying there peacefully, the father looked up at his son. "I know you are going to throw me over the cliff, but before you do, may I suggest something?"

"What is it?" replied the son.

"Throw me over the cliff, if you like," said the father, "but save this good wood coffin. Your children might need to use it."

Reflection: What goes around, comes around. The wise man always wins in the end, even in the worst of circumstances.

13. *The Gift of Insults*

There once lived a great warrior. Though quite old, he still was able to defeat any challenger. His reputation extended far and wide throughout the land and many students gathered to study under him.

One day an infamous young warrior arrived at the village. He was determined to be the first man to defeat the great master.

Along with his strength, he had an uncanny ability to spot and exploit any weakness in an opponent. He would wait for his opponent to make the first move, thus revealing a weakness, and then would strike with merciless force and lightning speed. No one had ever lasted with him in a match beyond the first move.

Much against the advice of his concerned students, the old master gladly accepted the young warrior's challenge.

As the two squared off for battle, the young warrior began to hurl insults at the old master. He threw dirt and spit in his face. For hours he verbally assaulted him with every curse and insult known to mankind. But the old warrior merely stood there motionless and calm. Finally, the young warrior exhausted himself.

Knowing he was defeated, he left feeling shamed.

Somewhat disappointed that he did not fight the insolent youth, the students gathered around the old master and questioned him. "How could you endure such an indignity? How did you drive him away?"

"If someone comes to give you a gift and you do not receive it," the master replied, "to whom does the gift belong?"

Reflection: There is no need to get even with people when you know you can actually get ahead of them.

14. *When Tired*

A student once asked this teacher, "Master, What is Enlightenment?"

The master replied, "When hungry, eat. When Tired, sleep".

Reflection: Living in the now is the most difficult task for us humans. Most live in the past or the future. Pleasures are simple things. Make the most of what you have.

15. *Transcient*

A famous spiritual teacher came to the front door of the king's palace. None of the guards tried to stop him as he entered and made his way to where the king himself was sitting on his throne.

"What do you want?", asked the king, immediately recognizing the visitor.

"I would like a place to sleep in this inn". Replied the teacher.

"But, this is not an inn,", said the king. "It's my palace".

"May I ask who owned this palace before you?"

"My father. He is dead".

"And who owned it before him?".

"My grand-father. He too is dead".

"And this place is where people live for a short time, and move on – did I hear you say that it is not an inn?"

Reflection: We are all here for just a short time, and then move on. Nothing in life is permanent. Materialism and wealth makes you think will last forever. It's all defense against the realization that everything eventually passes away.

16. *The Holy Man*

Once upon a time, in a countryside, word spread across about the wise Holy Man who lived in a small house atop the mountain.

A man from the village decided to make the long and difficult journey to visit him.

When he arrived at the house, he saw an old servant inside who greeted him at the door.

"I would like to see the wise Holy Man," he said to the servant.

The servant smiled and led him inside.

As they walked through the house, the man from the village looked eagerly around the house, anticipating his encounter with the Holy Man.

Before he knew it, he had been led to the back door and escorted outside.

He stopped and turned to the servant, "But I want to see the Holy Man!"

"You already have," said the old man.

"Everyone you may meet in life, even if they appear plain and insignificant... see each of them as a wise Holy Man. If you do this, then whatever problem you brought here today will be solved."

Reflection: Don't judge people until you get to know them. They may surprise you. If you feel love and respect for all people that you meet, you will receive inward peace.

17. *May Be*

There is a Taoist story of an old farmer who had worked his crops for many years. One day his horse ran away. Upon hearing the news, his neighbors came to visit.

"Such bad luck," they said sympathetically.

"May be," the farmer replied.

The next morning the horse returned, bringing with it three other wild horses.

"How wonderful," the neighbors exclaimed.

"May be," replied the old man.

The following day, his son tried to ride one of the untamed horses, was thrown, and broke his leg.

The neighbors again came to offer their sympathy on his misfortune.

"May be," answered the farmer.

The day after, military officials came to the village to draft young men into the army. Seeing that the son's leg was broken, they passed him by.

The neighbors congratulated the farmer on how well things had turned out.

"May be," said the farmer.

Reflection: Non–attachment is a way to rid your life of unnecessary unhappiness. It's a way to become happier. Human beings get attached to ideas – ideas about who they are, what's the best way to live, ideas about what other people should be like, and so on. and our attachment to those ideas causes most of our day to day suffering. It is our ideas about reality that causes the suffering. Not the reality itself.

18. <u>Nothing Exists</u>

Yamaoka Tesshu, as a young student of Zen, visited one master after another. He called upon Dokuon of Shokoku.

Desiring to show his attainment, he said: "The mind, Buddha, and sentient beings, after all, do not exist. The true nature of phenomena is emptiness. There is no realization, no delusion, no sage, no mediocrity. There is no giving and nothing to be received."

Dokuon, who was smoking quietly, said nothing. Suddenly he whacked Yamaoka with his bamboo pipe. This made the youth quite angry.

"If nothing exists," inquired Dokuon, "where did this anger come from?"

Reflection: When you take conscious control of all your decisions, you are actually activating certain neural pathways in your brain that help promote self-control, calmness and inner peace. Everytime you allow others to dictate your decisions or you don't take full conscious responsibility for your decisions, you become slightly conditioned to be less conscious when making choices.

19. *A Drop of Water*

A Zen master named Gisan asked a young student to bring him a pail of water to cool his bath.

The student brought the water and, after cooling the bath, threw on to the ground the little that was left over.

"You dunce!" the master scolded him. "Why didn't you give the rest of the water to the plants? What right have you to waste even one drop of water in this temple?"

The young student attained Zen in that instant. He changed his name to Tekisui, which means a drop of water.

Reflection – No matter where you are in your life journey at this moment, there are things around you that you should be enjoying and celebrating. If you were to sit down and marvel at how far you have come, appreciate the people who are currently in your life, and be amazed at how much you actually have, you would be in awe. One of the keys to enjoying your life is to take time to enjoy all the little things.

20. *Sounds of Silence*

The pupils of the Tendai school used to study meditation before Zen entered Japan. Four of them who were intimate friends promised one another to observe seven days of silence.

On the first day all were silent. Their meditation had begun auspiciously, but when night came and the oil lamps were growing dim one of the pupils could not help exclaiming to a servant: "Fix those lamps."

The second pupils was surprised to hear the first one talk. "We are not supposed to say a word," he remarked.

"You two are stupid. Why did you talk?" asked the third.

"I am the only one who has not talked," concluded the fourth pupil.

Reflection: Oaths and promises are lightly spoken - hardly kept. Try to keep the promises you make, otherwise you will lose your credibility.

21. *It will Pass*

A student went to his meditation teacher and said, "My meditation is horrible! I feel so distracted, or my legs ache, or I'm constantly falling asleep. It's just horrible!"

"It will pass," the teacher said matter-of-factly.

A week later, the student came back to his teacher.

"My meditation is wonderful! I feel so aware, so peaceful, so alive! It's just wonderful!'

"It will pass," the teacher replied matter-of-factly.

Reflection: It is true that the only constant in life is change. Life has its ups and downs – good days and bad; rain and sun, illness and health, laughter and tears – Nothing bad will last forever. Nothing good will last forever either.

22. *Practice makes Perfect*

A dramatic ballad singer studied under a strict teacher who insisted that he rehearse day after day, month after month the same passage from the same song, without being permitted to go any further.

Finally, overwhelmed by frustration and despair, the young man ran off to find another profession.

One night, stopping at an inn, he stumbled upon a recitation contest.

Having nothing to lose, he entered the competition and, of course, sang the one passage that he knew so well.

When he had finished, the sponsor of the contest highly praised his performance.

Despite the student's embarrassed objections, the sponsor refused to believe that he had just heard a beginner perform.

"Tell me," the sponsor said, "who is your instructor? He must be a great master."

The student later became known as the great performer Koshiji.

Reflection: The ballad singer practiced so much that it became a part of him. To really master something, it has to become part of you. Hard work will always pay off sometime in the future. Reminds me of the movie "The Karate Kid".

23. *Wanting God*

A hermit was meditating by a river when a young man interrupted him.

"Master, I wish to become your disciple," said the man. "Why?" replied the hermit.

The young man thought for a moment. "Because I want to find God."

The master jumped up, grabbed him by the scruff of his neck, dragged him into the river, and plunged his head under water.

After holding him there for a minute, with him kicking and struggling to free himself, the master finally pulled him up out of the river.

The young man coughed up water and gasped to get his breath. When he eventually quieted down, the master spoke. "Tell me, what did you want most of all when you were under water."

"Air!" answered the man.

"Very well," said the master."Go home and come back to me when you want God as much as you just wanted air."

Reflection: If you truly want God, you must put all other wishes and needs aside. God must become the center of your life. Wishing, needing, wanting and desiring isn't seeking. You are a seeker only when you are willing to give everything you've got, even your own self

24. *In the hands of destiny*

A Japanese general decided to attack the enemy although he had only one-tenth the number of men the opposition commanded. He knew that he would win, but his soldiers were in doubt.

On the way he stopped at a Shinto shrine and told his men: "After I visit the shrine I will toss a coin. If heads comes, we will win; if tails, we will lose. Destiny holds us in her hand."

The general entered the shrine and offered a silent prayer. He came forth and tossed a coin. Heads appeared. His soldiers were so overjoyed and filled with confidence that they vigorously attached the enemy and were victorious.

"No one can change the hand of destiny," a lieutenant told the general after the battle.

"Indeed not," said the general, showing a coin which had heads on both sides.

Reflection - If you believe in yourself, you can accomplish anything. There is nothing like the power of positive thinking.

25. *Concentration*

This is an interesting story about how fear can rule one's life.

After winning several archery contests, the young and rather boastful champion challenged a Zen master who was renowned for his skill as an archer.

The young man demonstrated remarkable technical proficiency when he hit a distant bull's eye on his first try, and then split that arrow with his second shot.

"There," he said to the old man, "see if you can match that!" Undisturbed, the master did not draw his bow, but rather motioned for the young archer to follow him up the mountain.

Curious about the old fellow's intentions, the champion followed him high into the mountain until they reached a deep chasm spanned by a rather flimsy and shaky log.

Calmly stepping out onto the middle of the unsteady and certainly perilous bridge, the old master picked a far away tree as a target, drew his bow, and fired a clean, direct hit.

"Now it is your turn," he said as he gracefully stepped back onto the safe ground. Staring with terror into the seemingly bottomless and beckoning abyss, the young man could not force himself to step out onto the log, no less shoot at a target.

"You have much skill with your bow," the master said, sensing his challenger's predicament, "but you have little skill with the mind that lets loose the shot."

Reflection – There is a big difference between talent and a disciplined mind. A disciplined mind is the most crucial element in mastering an art.

26. *Just two Words*

There once was a monastery that was very strict. Following a vow of silence, no one was allowed to speak at all. But there was one exception to this rule.

Every ten years, the monks were permitted to speak just two words.

After spending his first ten years at the monastery, one monk went to the head monk. "It has been ten years," said the head monk. "What are the two words you would like to speak?"

"Bed... hard..." said the monk.
"I see," replied the head monk.

Ten years later, the monk returned to the head monk's office. "It has been ten more years," said the head monk. "What are the two words you would like to speak?"

"Food... stinks..." said the monk.
"I see," replied the head monk.

Yet another ten years passed and the monk once again met with the head monk who asked,

"What are your two words now, after these ten years?"
"I... quit!" said the monk.

"Well, I can see why," replied the head monk. "All you ever do is complain."

Reflection: If you have a burning desire to learn or improve on something, just act, and do not complain.

27. *Banishing a Ghost*

A young wife fell sick and was about to die. "I love you so much," she told her husband, "I do not want to leave you. Do not go from me to any other woman. If you do, I will return as a ghost and cause you endless trouble."

Soon the wife passed away. The husband respected her last wish for the first three months, but then he met another woman and fell in love with her. They became engaged to be married.

Immediately after the engagement a ghost appeared every night to the man, blaming him for not keeping his promise. The ghost was clever too. She told him exactly what has transpired between himself and his new sweetheart. Whenever he gave his fiancee a present, the ghost would describe it in detail. She would even repeat conversations, and it so annoyed the man that he could not sleep. Someone advised him to take his problem to a Zen master who lived close to the village. At length, in despair, the poor man went to him for help.

"Your former wife became a ghost and knows everything you do," commented the master. "Whatever you do or say, whatever you give you beloved, she knows. She must be a very wise ghost. Really you should admire such a ghost. The next time she appears, bargain with her. Tell her that she knows so much you can hide nothing from her, and that if she will answer you one question, you promise to break your engagement and remain single."

"What is the question I must ask her?" inquired the man.

The master replied: "Take a large handful of soy beans and ask her exactly how many beans you hold in your hand. If she cannot tell you, you will know she is only a figment of your imagination and will trouble you no longer."

The next night, when the ghost appeared the man flattered her and told her that she knew everything.

"Indeed," replied the ghost, "and I know you went to see that Zen master today."

"And since you know so much," demanded the man, "tell me how many beans I hold in this hand!"

There was no longer any ghost to answer the question.

Reflection - The reason something haunts us is because we keep our attention on it. When we move on beyond it, it will disappear.

28. <u>*Muddy Road*</u>

Tanzan and Ekido were once travelling together down a muddy road. A heavy rain was still falling.

Coming around a bend, they met a lovely girl in a silk kimono and sash, unable to cross the intersection.

"Come on, girl," said Tanzan at once. Lifting her in his arms, he carried her over the mud.

Ekido did not speak again until that night when they reached a lodging temple. Then he no longer could restrain himself. "We monks don't do near females," he told Tanzan, "especially not young and lovely ones. It is dangerous. Why did you do that?"

"I left the girl there," said Tanzan. "Are you still carrying her?"

Reflection - We all carry with us the weight of our past mistakes, regrets and mistaken beliefs. If you are clearly in control of your mind, nothing that comes in the way can stop your progress.

29. *Is that so?*

The Zen master Hakuin was praised by his neighbors as one living a pure life.

A beautiful Japanese girl whose parents owned a food store lived near him. Suddenly, without any warning, her parents discovered she was with child.

This made her parents very angry. She would not confess who the man was, but after much harassment at last named Hakuin.

In great anger the parents went to the master. "Is that so?" was all he would say.

After the child was born it was brought to Hakuin. By this time he had lost his reputation, which did not trouble him, but he took very good care of the child. He obtained milk from his neighbors and everything else the little one needed.

A year later the girl-mother could stand it no longer. She told her parents the truth - that the real father of the child was a young man who worked in the fishmarket.

The mother and father of the girl at once went to Hakuin to ask his forgiveness, to apologize at length, and to get the child back again.

Hakuin was willing. In yielding the child, all he said was: "Is that so?"

Reflection - People saying something does not make it true. Knowing yourself is the most important thing.

30. *Empty your Cup*

Nan-in, a Japanese master during the Meiji era (1868-1912), received a university professor who came to inquire about Zen. Nan-in served tea. He poured his visitor's cup full, and then kept on pouring.

The professor watched the overflow until he no longer could restrain himself. "It is overfull. No more will go in!"

"Like this cup," Nan-in said, "you are full of your own opinions and speculations. How can I show you Zen unless you first empty your cup?"

Reflection - Preconceived ideas and prejudices always prevent us from seeing the truth.

CHAPTER TWO

ZEN STORIES: 1-50

1. A Cup of Tea

Nan-in, a Japanese master during the Meiji era (1868-1912), received a university professor who came to inquire about Zen.

Nan-in served tea. He poured his visitor's cup full, and then kept on pouring.

The professor watched the overflow until he no longer could restrain himself. "It is overfull. No more will go in!"

"Like this cup," Nan-in said, "you are full of your own opinions and speculations. How can I show you Zen unless you first empty your cup?"

2. Finding a Diamond on a Muddy Road

Gudo was the emperor's teacher of his time. Nevertheless, he used to travel alone as a wandering mendicant. Once when he was on his was to Edo, the cultural and political center of the shogunate, he approached a little village named Takenaka. It was evening and a heavy rain was falling. Gudo was thoroughly wet. His straw sandals were in pieces. At a farmhouse near the village he noticed four or five pairs of sandals in the window and decided to buy some dry ones.

The woman who offered him the sandals, seeing how wet he was, invited him in to remain for the night at her home. Gudo accepted, thanking her. He entered and recited a sutra before the family shrine. He then was introduced to the woman's mother, and to her children. Observing that the entire family was depressed, Gudo asked what was wrong.

"My husband is a gambler and a drunkard," the housewife told him. "When he happens to win he drinks and becomes abusive. When he loses he borrows money from others. Sometimes when he becomes thoroughly drunk he does not come home at all. What can I do?"

I will help him," said Gudo. "Here is some money. Get me a gallon of fine wine and something good to eat. Then you may retire. I will meditate before the shrine."

When the man of the house returned about midnight, quite drunk, he bellowed: "Hey, wife, I am home. Have you something for me to eat?"

"I have something for you," said Gudo. "I happened to get caught in the rain and your wife kindly asked me to remain here for the night. In return I have bought some wine and fish, so you might as well have them."

The man was delighted. He drank the wine at once and laid himself down on the floor. Gudo sat in meditation beside him.

In the morning when the husband awoke he had forgotten about the previous night. "Who are you? Where do you come from?" he asked Gudo, who still was meditating.

"I am Gudo of Kyoto and I am going on to Edo," replied the Zen master.

The man was utterly ashamed. He apologized profusely to the teacher of his emperor.

Gudo smiled. "Everything in this life is impermanent," he explained. "Life is very brief. If you keep on gambling and drinking, you will have no time left to accomplish anything else, and you will cause your family to suffer too."

The perception of the husband awoke as if from a dream. "You are right," he declared. "How can I ever repay you for this wonderful teaching! Let me see you off and carry your things a little way."

"If you wish," assented Gudo.

The two started out. After they had gone three miles Gudo told him to return. "Just another five miles," he begged Gudo. They continued on.

"You may return now," suggested Gudo.

"After another ten miles," the man replied.

"Return now," said Gudo, when the ten miles had been passed.

"I am going to follow you all the rest of my life," declared the man.

Modern Zen teachers in Japan spring from the lineage of a famous master who was the successor of Gudo. His name was Mu-nan, the man who never turned back.

3. Is That So?

The Zen master Hakuin was praised by his neighbors as one living a pure life.

A beautiful Japanese girl whose parents owned a food store lived near him. Suddenly, without any warning, her parents discovered she was with child.

This made her parents very angry. She would not confess who the man was, but after much harassment at last named Hakuin.

In great anger the parents went to the master. "Is that so?" was all he would say.

After the child was born it was brought to Hakuin. By this time he had lost his reputation, which did not trouble him, but he took very good care of the child. He obtained milk from his neighbors and everything else the little one needed.

A year later the girl-mother could stand it no longer. She told her parents the truth - that the real father of the child was a young man who worked in the fishmarket.

The mother and father of the girl at once went to Hakuin to ask his forgiveness, to apologize at length, and to get the child back again.

Hakuin was willing. In yielding the child, all he said was: "Is that so?"

4. Obedience

The master Bankei's talks were attended not only by Zen students but by persons of all ranks and sects. He never quoted sutras nor indulged in scholastic dissertations. Instead, his words were spoken directly from his heart to the hearts of his listeners.

His large audiences angered a priest of the Nichiren sect because the adherents had left to hear about Zen. The self-centered Nichiren priest came to the temple, determined to debate with Bankei.

"Hey, Zen teacher!" he called out. "Wait a minute. Whoever respects you will obey what you say, but a man like myself does not respect you. Can you make me obey you?"

"Come up beside me and I will show you," said Bankei.

Proudly the priest pushed his way through the crowd to the teacher.

Bankei smiled. "Come over to my left side."

The priest obeyed.

"No," said Bankei, "we may talk better if you are on the right side. Step over here."

The priest proudly stepped over to the right

"You see," observed Bankei, "you are obeying me and I think you are a very gentle person. Now sit down and listen."

5. *If You Love, Love Openly*

Twenty monks and one nun, who was named Eshun, were practicing meditation with a certain Zen master.

Eshun was very pretty even though her head was shaved and her dress plain. Several monks secretly fell in love with her. One of them wrote her a love letter, insisting upon a private meeting.

Eshun did not reply. The following day the master gave a lecture to the group, and when it was over, Eshun arose. Addressing the one who had written her, she said: "If you really love me so much, come and embrace me now."

6. *No Loving - Kindness*

There was an old woman in China who had supported a monk for over twenty years. She had built a little hut for him and fed him while he was meditating. Finally she wondered just what progress he had made in all this time.

To find out, she obtained the help of a girl rich in desire. "Go and embrace him," she told her, "and then ask him suddenly: 'What now?'"

The girl called upon the monk and without much ado caressed him, asking him what he was going to do about it.

"An old tree grows on a cold rock in winter," replied the monk somewhat poetically. "Nowhere is there any warmth."

The girl returned and related what he had said.

"To think I fed that fellow for twenty years!" exclaimed the old woman in anger. "He showed no consideration for your need, no disposition to explain your condition. He need not have responded to passion, but at least he could have evidenced some compassion;"

She at once went to the hut of the monk and burned it down.

7. Annoucement

Tanzan wrote sixty postal cards on the last day of his life, and asked an attendant to mail them. Then he passed away.

The cards read:

I am departing from this world.

This is my last announcement.

Tanzan

July 27, 1892

8. Great Waves

In the early days of the Meiji era there lived a well-known wrestler called O-nami, Great Waves.

O-nami was immensly strong and knew the art of wresting. In his private bouts he defeated even his teacher, but in public was so bashful that his own pupils threw him.

O-nami felt he should go to a Zen master for help. Hakuju, a wandering teacher, was stopping in a little temple nearby, so O-nami went to see him and told him of his great trouble.

"Great Waves is your name," the teacher advised, "so stay in this temple tonight. Imagine that you are those billows. You are no longer a wrestler who is afraid. You are those huge waves sweeping everything before them, swallowing all in their path. Do this and you will be the greatest wrestler in the land."

The teacher retired. O-nami sat in meditation trying to imagine himself as waves. He thought of many different things. Then gradualy he turned more and more to the feeling of waves. As the night advanced the waves became larger and larger. They swept away the flowers in their vases. Even the Buddha in the shrine was inundated. Before dawn the temple was nothing but the ebb and flow of an immense sea.

In the morning the teacher found O-nami meditating, a faint smile on his face. He patted the wrestler's shoulder. "Now nothing can disturb you," he said. "You are those waves. You will sweep everything before you."

The same day O-nami entered the wrestling contests and won. After that, no one in Japan was able to defeat him.

9. *The Moon Cannot Be Stolen*

Ryokan, a Zen master, lived the simplest kind of life in a little hut at the foot of a mountain. One evening a thief visited the hut only to discover there was nothing in it to steal.

Ryokan returned and caught him. "You may have come a long way to visit me," he told the prowler, "and you shoud not return emptyhanded. Please take my clothes as a gift."

The thief was bewildered. He took the clothes and slunk away.

Ryokan sat naked, watching the moon. "Poor fellow, " he mused, "I wish I could give him this beautiful moon."

10. *The Last Poem of Hoshin*

The Zen master Hoshin lived in China many years. Then he returned to the northeastern part of Japan, where he taught his disciples. When he was getting very old, he told them a story he had heard in China. This is the story:

One year on the twenty-fifth of December, Tokufu, who was very old, said to his disciples: "I am not going to be alive next year so you fellows should treat me well this year."

The pupils thought he was joking, but since he was a great-hearted teacher each of them in turn treated him to a feast on succeeding days of the departing year.

On the eve of the new year, Tokufu concluded: "You have been good to me. I shall leave you tomorrow afternoon when the snow has stopped."

The disciples laughed, thinking he was aging and talking nonsense since the night was clear and without snow. But at midnight snow began to fall, and the next day they did not find their teacher about. They went to the meditation hall. There he had passed on.

Hoshin, who related this story, told his disciples: "It is not necessary for a Zen master to predict his passing, but if he really wishes to do so, he can."

"Can you?" someone asked.

"Yes," answered Hoshin. "I will show you what I can do seven days from now."

None of the disciples believed him, and most of them had even forgotten the conversation when Hoshin next called them together.

"Seven days ago," he remarked, "I said I was going to leave you. It is customary to write a farewell poem, but I am neither poet nor calligrapher. Let one of you inscribe my last words."

His followers thought he was joking, but one of them started to write.

"Are you ready?" Hoshin asked.

"Yes, sir," replied the writer.

Then Hoshin dictated:

I came from brilliancy.

And return to brilliancy.

What is this?

The poem was one line short of the customary four, so the disciple said: "Master, we are one line short."

Hoshin, with the roar of a conquoring lion, shouted "Kaa!" and was gone.

11. The Story of Shunkai

The exquisite Shunkai whose other name was Suzu was compelled to marry against her wishes when she was quite young. Later, after this marriage had ended, she attended the university, where she studied philosophy.

To see Shunkai was to fall in love with her. Moreover, wherever she went, she herself fell in love with others. Love was with her at the university, and afterwards, when philosophy did not satisfy her and she visited a temple to learn about Zen, the Zen students fell in love with her. Shunkai's whole life was saturated with love.

At last in Kyoto she became a real student of Zen. Her brothers in the sub-temple of Kennin praised her sincerity. One of them proved to be a congenial spirit and assisted her in the mastery of Zen.

The abbot of Kennin, Mokurai, Silent Thunder, was severe. He kept the precepts himself and expected his priests to do so. In modern Japan whatever zeal these priests have lost of Buddhism they seem to have gained for their wives. Mokurai used to take a broom and chase the women away when he found them in any of his temples, but the more wives he swept out, the more seemed to come back.

In this particular temple the wife of the head priest became jealous of Shunkai's earnestness and beauty. Hearing the students praise her serious Zen made this wife squirm and itch. Finally she spread a rumor about Shunkai and the young man who was her friend. As a consequence he was expelled and Shunkai was removed from the temple.

"I may have made the mistake of love," thought Shunkai, "but the priest's wife shall not remain in the temple either if my friend is to be treated so unjustly."

Shunkai the same night with a can of kerosene set fire to the five-hundred-year-old temple and burned it to the ground. In the morning she found herself in the hands of the police.

A young lawyer became interested in her and endeavored to make her sentence lighter. "Do not help me," she told him. "I might decide to do something else which would only imprison me again."

At last a sentence of seven years was completed, and Shunkai was released from the prison, where the sixty-year-old warden had become enamored of her.

But now everyone looked upon her as a "jailbird." No one would associate with her. Even the Zen people, who are supposed to believe in enlightenment in this life and with this body, shunned her. Zen, Shunkai found, was one thing and the followers of Zen quite another. Her relatives would have nothing to do with her. She grew sick, poor, and weak.

She met a Shinshu priest who taught her the name of the Buddha of Love, and in this Shunkai found some solace and peace of mind. She passed away when she was still exquisitely beautiful and hardly thirty years old.

She wrote her own story in a futile endeavor to support herself and some of it she told to a woman writer. So it reached the Japanese people. Those who rejected Shunkai, those who slandered and hated her, now read of her live with tears of remorse.

12. Happy Chinaman

Anyone walking about Chinatowns in America will observe statues of a stout fellow carrying a linen sack. Chinese merchants call him Happy Chinaman or Laughing Buddha.

This Hotei lived in the T'ang dynasty. He had no desire to call himself a Zen master or to gather many disciples around him. Instead he walked the streets with a big sack into which he would put gifts of candy, fruit, or doughnuts. These he would give to children who gathered around him in play. He established a kindergarten of the streets.

Whenever he met a Zen devotee he would extend his hand and say: "Give me one penny."

Once as he was about to play-work another Zen master happened along and inquired: "What is the significance of Zen?"

Hotei immediately plopped his sack down on the ground in silent answer.

"Then," asked the other, "what is the actualization of Zen?"

At once the Happy Chinaman swung the sack over his shoulder and continued on his way.

13. A Buddha

In Tokyo in the Meiji era there lived two prominent teachers of opposite characteristics. One, Unsho, an instructor in Shingon, kept Buddha's precepts scrupulously. He never drank intoxicants, nor did he eat after eleven o'clock in the morning. The other teacher, Tanzan, a professor of philosophy at the Imperial University, never observed the precepts. When he felt like eating, he ate, and when he felt like sleeping in the daytime, he slept.

One day Unsho visited Tanzan, who was drinking wine at the time, not even a drop of which is supposed to touch the tongue of a Buddhist.

"Hello, brother," Tanzan greeted him. "Won't you have a drink?"

"I never drink!" exclaimed Unsho solemnly.

"One who does not drink is not even human," said Tanzan.

"Do you mean to call me inhuman just because I do not indulge in intoxicating liquids!" exclaimed Unsho in anger. "Then if I am not human, what am I?"

"A Buddha," answered Tanzan.

14. Muddy Road

Tanzan and Ekido were once travelling together down a muddy road. A heavy rain was still falling.

Coming around a bend, they met a lovely girl in a silk kimono and sash, unable to cross the intersection.

"Come on, girl," said Tanzan at once. Lifting her in his arms, he carried her over the mud.

Ekido did not speak again until that night when they reached a lodging temple. Then he no longer could restrain himself. "We monks don't do near females," he told Tanzan, "especially not young and lovely ones. It is dangerous. Why did you do that?"

"I left the girl there," said Tanzan. "Are you still carrying her?"

15. Shoan and His Mother

Shoun became a teacher of Soto Zen. When he was still a student his father passed away, leaving him to care for his old mother.

Whenever Shoun went to a meditation hall he always took his mother with him. Since she accompanied him, when he visited monasteries he could not live with the monks. So he would build a little house and care for her there. He would copy sutras, Buddhist verses, and in this manner receive a few coins for food.

When Shoun bought fish for his mother, the people would scoff at him, for a monk is not supposed to eat fish. But Shoun did not mind. His mother, however, was hurt to see the others laugh at her son. Finally she told Shoun: "I think I will become a nun. I can be a vegaterian too." She did, and they studied together.

Shoun was fond of music and was a master of the harp, which his mother also played. On full-moon nights they used to play together.

One night a young lady passed by their house and heard music. Deeply touched, she invited Shoun to visit her the next evening and play. He accepted the invitation. A few days later he met the young lady on the street and thanked her for her hospitality. Others laughed at him. He had visited the house of a woman of the streets.

One day Shoun left for a distant temple to deliver a lecture. A few months afterwards he returned home to find his mother dead. Friends had not known where to reach him, so the funeral was then in progress.

Shoun walked up and hit the coffin with his staff. "Mother, your son has returned," he said.

"I am glad to see you have returned, son," he answered for his mother.

"Yes, I am glad too," Shoun responded. Then he announced to the people about him: "The funeral ceremony is over. You may bury the body."

When Shoun was old he knew his end was approaching. He asked his disciples to gather around him in the morning, telling them he was going to pass on at noon. Burning incense before the picture of his mother and his old teacher, he wrote a poem:

For fifty-six years I lived as best I could,
Making my way in this world.

Now the rain has ended, the clouds are clearing,
The blue sky has a full moon.

His disciples gathered about him, reciting a sutra, and Shoun passed on during the invocation.

16. Not Far From Buddhahood

A university student while visiting Gasan asked him: "Have you even read the Christian Bible?"

"No, read it to me," said Gasan.

The student opened the Bible and read from St. Matthew: "And why take ye thought for raiment? Consider the lilies of the field, how they grow. They toil not, neither do they spin, and yet I say unto you that even Solomon in all his glory was not arrayed like one of these...Take therefore no thought for the morrow, for the morrow shall take thought for the things of itself."

Gasan said: "Whoever uttered those words I consider and enlightened man."

The student continued reading: "Ask and it shall be given you, seek and ye shall find, knock and it shall be opened unto you. For everyone that asketh receiveth, and he that seeketh findeth, and to him that knocketh, is shall be opened."

Gasan remarked: "That is excellent. Whoever said that is not far from Buddhahood."

17. Stingy in Teaching

A young physician in Tokyo named Kusuda met a college friend who had been studying Zen. The young doctor asked him what Zen was.

"I cannot tell you what it is," the friend replied, "but one thing is certain. If you understand Zen, you will not be afraid to die."

"That's fine," said Kusuda. "I will try it. Where can I find a teacher?"

"Go to the master Nan-in," the friend told him.

So Kusuda went to call on Nan-in. He carried a dagger nine and a half inches long to determine whether or not the teacher was afraid to die.

When Nan-in saw Kusuda he exclaimed: "Hello, friend. How are you? We haven't seen each other for a long time!"

This perplexed Kusuda, who replied: "We have never met before."

"That's right," answered Nan-in. "I mistook you for another physician who is receiving instruction here."

With such a beginning, Kusuda lost his chance to test the master, so reluctantly he asked if he might receive Zen instruction.

Nan-in said: "Zen is not a difficult task. If you are a physician, treat you patients with kindness. That is Zen."

Kusuda visited Nan-in three times. Each time Nan-in told him the same thing. "A physician should not waste time around here. Go home and take care of you patients."

It was not yet clear to Kusuda how such teaching could remove the fear of death. So on his fourth visit he complained: "My friend told me when one learns Zen one loses the fear of death. Each time I come here all you tell me is to take care of my patients. I know that much. If that is your so-called Zen, I am not going to visit you any more."

Nan-in smiled and patted the doctor. "I have been too strict with you. Let me give you a koan." He presented Kusuda with Joshu's Mu to work over, which is the first mind enlightening problem in the book called The Gateless Gate.

Kusuda pondered this problem of Mu (No-Thing) for two years. At length he thought he had reached certainty of mind. But his teacher commented: "You are not in yet."

Kusuda continued in concentration for another year and a half. His mind became placid. Problems dissolved. No-Thing became the truth. He served his patients well and, without even knowing it, he was free from concern over life and death.

Then when he visited Nan-in, his old teacher just smiled.

18. A Parable

Buddha told a parable in a sutra:

A man traveling across a field encountered a tiger. He fled, the tiger after him. Coming to a precipice, he caught hold of the root of a wild vine and swung himself down over the edge. The tiger sniffed at him from above. Trembling, the man looked down to where, far below, another tiger was waiting to eat him. Only the vine sustained him.

Two mice, one white and one black, little by little started to gnaw away the vine. The man saw a luscious strawberry near him. Grasping the vine with one hand, he plucked the strawberry with the other. How sweet it tasted!

19. The First Principle

When one goes to Obaku temple in Kyoto he sees carved over the gate the words "The First Principle". The letters are unusually large, and those who appreciate calligraphy always admire them as being a mastepiece. They were drawn by Kosen two hundred years ago.

When the master drew them he did so on paper, from which the workmen made the large carving in wood. As Kosen sketched the letters a bold pupil was with him who had made several gallons of ink for the calligraphy and who never failed to criticise his master's work.

"That is not good," he told Kosen after his first effort.

"How is this one?"

"Poor. Worse than before," pronounced the pupil.

Kosen patiently wrote one sheet after another until eighty-four First Principles had accumulated, still without the approval of the puil.

Then when the young man stepped outside for a few moments, Kosen thought: "Now this is my chance to escape his keen eye," and he wrote hurriedly, with a mind free from distraction: "The First Principle."

"A masterpiece," pronounced the pupil.

20. A Mother's Advice

Jiun, a Shogun master, was a well-known Sanskrit scholar of the Tokugawa era. When he was young he used to deliver lectures to his brother students.

His mother heard about this and wrote him a letter.:

"Son, I do not think you became a devotee of the Buddha because you desired to turn into a walking dictionary for others. There is no end to information and commentation, glory and honor. I wish you would stop this lecture business. Shut yourself up in a little temple in a remote part of the mountain. Devote your time to meditation and in this way attain true realization."

21. The Sound of One Hand

The master of Kennin temple was Mokurai, Silent Thunder. He had a little protégé named Toyo who was only twelve years old. Toyo saw the older disciples visit the master's room each morning and evening to receive instruction in sanzen or personal guidence in which they were given koans to stop mind-wandering.

Toyo wished to do sanzen also.

"Wait a while," said Mokurai. "You are too young."

But the child insisted, so the teacher finally consented.

In the evening little Toyo went at the proper time to the threshold of Mokurai's sanzen room. He struck the gong to announce his presence, bowed respectfully three times outside the door, and went to sit before the master in respectful silence.

"You can hear the sound of two hands when they clap together," said Mokurai. "Now show me the sound of one hand."

Toyo bowed and went to his room to consider this problem. From his window he could hear the music of the geishas. "Ah, I have it!" he proclaimed.

The next evening, when his teacher asked him to illustrate the sound of one hand, Toyo began to play the music of the geishas.

"No, no," said Mokurai. "That will never do. That is not the sound of one hand. You've not got it at all."

Thinking that such music might interrupt, Toyo moved his abode to a quiet place. He meditated again. "What can the sound of one hand be?" He happened to hear some water dripping. "I have it," imagined Toyo.

Whcn he next appeared before his teacher, he imitated dripping water.

"What is that?" asked Mokurai. "That is the sound of dripping water, but not the sound of one hand. Try again."

In vain Toyo meditated to hear the sound of one hand. He heard the sighing of the wind. But the sound was rejected.

He heard the cry of an owl. This was also refused.

The sound of one hand was not the locusts.

For more than ten times Toyo visited Mokurai with different sounds. All were wrong. For almost a year he pondered what the sound of one hand might be.

At last Toyo entered true meditation and transcended all sounds. "I could collect no more," he explained later, "so I reached the soundless sound."

Toyo had realized the sound of one hand.

22. *My Heart Burns Like Fire*

Soyen Shaku, the first Zen teacher to come to America, said: "My heart burns like fire but my eyes are as cold as dead ashes." He made the following rules which he practiced every day of his life.

•In the morning before dressing, light incense and meditate.

• Retire at a regular hour. Partake of food at regular intervals. Eat with moderation and never to the point of satisfaction.

• Receive a guest with the same attitude you have when alone. When alone, maintain the same attitude you have in receiving guests.

• Watch what you say, and whatever you say, practice it.

• When an opportunity comes do not let it pass you by, yet always think twice before acting.

•Do not regret the past. Look to the future.

• Have the fearless attitude of a hero and the loving heart of a child.

• Upon retiring, sleep as if you had entered your last sleep. Upon awakening, leave your bed behind you instantly as if you had cast away a pair of old shoes.

23. *Eshun's Departure*

When Eshun, the Zen nun, was past sixty and about to leave this world, she asked some monks to pile up wood in the yard.

Seating herself firmly in the center of the funeral pyre, she had it set fire around the edges.

"O nun!" shouted one monk, "is it hot in there?"

"Such a matter would concern only a stupid person like yourself," answered Eshun.

The flames arose, and she passed away.

24. *Reciting Sutras*

A farmer requested a Tendai priest to recite sutras for his wife, who had died. After the recitation was over the farmer asked: "Do you think my wife will gain merit from this?"

"Not only your wife, but all sentient beings will benefit from the recitation of sutras," answered the priest.

"If you say all sentient beings will benefit," said the farmer, "my wife may be very weak and others will take advantage of her, getting the benefit she should have. So please recite sutras just for her."

The priest explained that it was the desire of a Buddhist to offer blessings and wish merit for every living being.

"That is a fine teaching," concluded the farmer, "but please make one exception. I have a neighbor who is rough and mean to me. Just exclude him from all those sentient beings."

25. Three Days More

Suiwo, the disciple of Hakuin, was a good teacher. During one summer seclusion period, a pupil came to him from a southern island of Japan.

Suiwo gave him the problem: "Hear the sound of one hand."

The pupil remained three years but could not pass the test. One night he came in tears to Suiwo. "I must return south in shame and embarrassment," he said, "for I cannot solve my problem."

"Wait one week more and meditate constantly," advised Suiwo. Still no enlightenment came to the pupil. "Try for another week," said Suiwo. The pupil obeyed, but in vain.

"Still another week." Yet this was of no avail. In despair the student begged to be released, but Suiwo requested another meditation of five days. They were without result. Then he said: "Meditate for three days longer, then if you fail to attain enlightenment, you had better kill yourself."

On the second day the pupil was enlightened.

26. Trading Dialogue For Lodging

Provided he makes and wins an argument about Buddhism with those who live there, any wandering monk can remain in a Zen temple. If he is defeated, he has to move on.

In a temple in the northern part of Japan two brother monks were dwelling together. The elder one was learned, but the younger one was stupid and had but one eye.

A wandering monk came and asked for lodging, properly challenging them to a debate about the sublime teaching. The elder brother, tired that day from much studying, told the younger one to take his place. "Go and request the dialogue in silence," he cautioned.

So the young monk and the stranger went to the shrine and sat down.

Shortly afterwards the traveler rose and went in to the elder brother and said: "Your young brother is a wonderful fellow. He defeated me."

"Relate the dialogue to me," said the elder one.

"Well," explained the traveler, "first I held up one finger, representing Buddha, the enlightened one. So he held up two fingers, signifying Buddha and his teaching. I held up three fingers, representing Buddha, his teaching, and his followers, living the harmonious life. Then he shook his clenched fist in my face, indicating that all three come from one realization. Thus he won and so I have no right to remain here." With this, the traveler left.

"Where is that fellow?" asked the younger one, running in to his elder brother.

"I understand you won the debate."

"Won nothing. I'm going to beat him up."

"Tell me the subject of the debate," asked the elder one.

"Why, the minute he saw me he held up one finger, insulting me by insinuating that I have only one eye. Since he was a stranger I thought I would be polite to him, so I held up two fingers, congratulating him that he has two eyes. Then the impolite wretch held up three fingers, suggesting that between us we only have three eyes. So I got mad and started to punch him, but he ran out and that ended it!"

27. The Voice of Happiness

After Bankei had passed away, a blind man who lived near the master's temple told a friend: "Since I am blind, I cannot watch a person's face, so I must judge his character by the sound of his voice. Ordinarily when I hear someone congratulate another upon his happiness or success, I also hear a secret tone of envy. When condolence is expressed for the misfortune of another, I hear pleasure and satisfaction, as if the one condoling was really glad there was something left to gain in his own world.

"In all my experience, however, Bankei's voice was always sincere. Whenever he expressed happiness, I heard nothing but happiness, and whenever he expressed sorrow, sorrow was all I heard."

28. *Open Your Own Treasure House*

Daiju visited the master Baso in China. Baso asked: "What do you seek?"

"Enlightenment," replied Daiju.

"You have your own treasure house. Why do you search outside?" Baso asked.

Daiju inquired: "Where is my treasure house?"

Baso answered: "What you are asking is your treasure house."

Daiju was delighted! Ever after he urged his friends: "Open your own treasure house and use those treasures."

29. *No Water, No Moon*

When the nun Chiyono studied Zen under Bukko of Engaku she was unable to attain the fruits of meditation for a long time.

At last one moonlit night she was carrying water in an old pail bound with bamboo. The bamboo broke and the bottom fell out of the pail, and at that moment Chiyono was set free!

In commemoration, she wrote a poem:

In this way and that I tried to save the old pail

Since the bamboo strip was weakening and about to break

Until at last the bottom fell out.

No more water in the pail!

No more moon in the water!

30. *Calling Card*

Keichu, the great Zen teacher of the Meiji era, was the head of Tofuku, a cathedral in Kyoto. One day the governor of Kyoto called upon him for the first time.

His attendant presented the card of the governor, which read: Kitagaki, Governor of Kyoto.

"I have no business with such a fellow," said Keichu to his attendant. "Tell him to get out of here."The attendant carried the card back with apologies. "That was my error," said the governor, and with a pencil he scratched out the words Governor of Kyoto. "Ask your teacher again."

"Oh, is that Kitagaki?" exclaimed the teacher when he saw the card. "I want to see that fellow."

31. Everything is Best

When Banzan was walking through a market he overheard a conversation between a butcher and his customer.

"Give me the best piece of meat you have," said the customer.

"Everything in my shop is the best," replied the butcher. "You cannot find here any piece of meat that is not the best."

At these words Banzan became enlightened.

32. Inch Time Foot Gem

A lord asked Takuan, a Zen teacher, to suggest how he might pass the time. He felt his days very long attending his office and sitting stiffly to receive the homage of others.

Takuan wrote eight Chinese characters and gave them to the man:

Not twice this day

Inch time foot gem.

This day will not come again.

Each minute is worth a priceless gem.

33. Mokusen's Hand

Mokusen Hiki was living in a temple in the province of Tamba. One of his adherents complained of the stinginess of his wife.

Mokusen visited the adherent's wife and showed her his clenched fist before her face.

"What do you mean by that?" asked the surprised woman.

"Suppose my fist were always like that. What would you call it?" he asked.

"Deformed," replied the woman.

The he opened his hand flat in her face and asked: "Suppose it were always like that. What then?"

"Another kind of deformity," said the wife.

"If you understand that much," finished Mokusen, "you are a good wife." Then he left.

After his visit, this wife helped her husband to distribute as well as to save.

34. A Smile in His Lifetime

Mokugen was never known to smile until his last day on earth. When his time came to pass away he said to his faithful ones: "You have studied under me for more than ten years. Show me your real interpretation of Zen. Whoever expresses this most clearly shall by my successor and receive my robe and bowl."

Everyone watched Mokugen's severe face, but no one answered.

Encho, a disciple who had been with his teacher for a long time, moved near the bedside. He pushed forward the medicine cup a few inches. This was his answer to the command.

The teacher's face became even more severe. "Is that all you understand?" he asked.

Encho reached out and moved the cup back again.

A beautiful smile broke over the features of Mokugen. "You rascal," he told Encho. "You worked with me ten years and have not yet seen my whole body. Take the robe and bowl. They belong to you."

35. Every-Minute Zen

Zen students are with their masters at least two years before they presume to teach others. Nan-in was visited by Tenno, who, having passed his apprenticeship, had become a teacher. The day happened to be rainy, so Tenno wore wodden clogs and carried an umbrella. After greeting him Nan-in remarked: "I suppose you left your wooden clogs in the vestibule. I want to know if your umbrella is on the right or left side of the clogs."

Tenno, confused, had no instant answer. He realized that he was unable to carry his Zen every minute. He became Nan-in's pupil, and he studied six more years to accomplish his every-minute Zen.

36. Flower Shower

Subhuti was Buddha's disciple. He was able to understand the potency of emptiness, the viewpoint that nothing exists except in its relationship of subjectivity and objectivity.

One day Subhuti, in a mood of sublime emptiness, was sitting under a tree. Flowers began to fall about him.

"We are praising you for your discourse on emptiness," the gods whispered to him.

"But I have not spoken of emptiness," said Subhuti.

"You have not spoken of emptiness, we have not heard emptiness," responded the gods. "This is true emptiness." And blossoms showered upon Subhuto as rain.

37. Publishing the Sutras

Tetsugen, a devotee of Zen in Japan, decided to publish the sutras, which at that time were available only in Chinese. The books were to be printed with wood blocks in an edition of seven thousand copies, a tremendous undertaking.

Tetsugen began by traveling and collecting donations for this purpose. A few sympathizers would give him a hundred pieces of gold, but most of the time he received only small coins. He thanked each donor with equal gratitude. After ten years Tetsugen had enough money to begin his task.

It happened that at that time the Uji River overflowed. Famine followed. Tetsugen took the funds he had collected for the books and spent them to save others from starvation. Then he began again his work of collecting.

Several years afterwards an epidemic spread over the country. Tetsugen again gave away what he had collected, to help his people.

For a third time he started his work, and after twenty years his wish was fulfilled. The printing blocks which produced the first edition of sutras can be seen today in the Obaku monastery in Kyoto.

The Japanese tell their children that Tetsugen made three sets of sutras, and that the first two invisible sets surpass even the last.

38. Gisho's Work

Gisho was ordained as a nun when she was ten years old. She received training just as the little boys did. When she reached the age of sixteen she traveled from one Zen master to another, studying with them all.

She remained three years with Unzan, six years with Gukei, but was unable to obtained a clear vision. At last she went to the master Inzan.

Inzan showed her no distinction at all on account of her sex. He scolded her like a thunderstorm. He cuffed her to awaken her inner nature.

Gisho remained with Inzan thirteen years, and then she found that which she was seeking!

In her honor, Inzan wrote a poem:

This nun studied thirteen years under my guidance.

In the evening she considered the deepest koans,

In the morning she was wrapped in other koans.

The Chinese nun Tetsuma surpassed all before her,

And since Mujaku none has been so genuine as this Gisho!

Yet there are many more gates for her to pass through.

She should receive still more blows from my iron fist.

After Gisho was enlightened she went to the province of Banshu, started her own Zen temple, and taught two hundred other nuns until she passed away one year in the month of August.

39. Sleeping in the Daytime

The master Soyen Shaku passed from this world when he was sixty-one years of age. Fulfilling his life's work, he left a great teaching, far richer than that of most Zen masters. His pupils used to sleep in the daytime during midsummer, and while he overlooked this he himself never wasted a minute.

When he was but twelve years old he was already studying Tendai philosophical speculation. One summer day the air had been so sultry that little Soyen stretched his legs and went to sleep while his teacher was away.

Three hours passed when, suddenly waking, he heard his master enter, but it was too late. There he lay, sprawled across the doorway.

"I beg your pardon, I beg your pardon," his teacher whispered, stepping carefully over Soyen's body as if it were that of some distinguished guest. After this, Soyen never slept again in the afternoon.

40. In Dreamland

"Our schoolmaster used to take a nap every afternoon," related a disciple of Soyen Shaku. "We children asked him why he did it and he told us: 'I go to dreamland to meet the old sages just as Confucius did.' When Confucius slept, he would dream of ancient sages and later tell his followers about them.

"It was extremely hot one day so some of us took a nap. Our schoolmaster scolded us. 'We went to dreamland to meet the ancient sages the same as Confucius did,' we explained. 'What was the message from those sages?' our schoolmaster demanded. One of us replied: 'We went to dreamland and met the sages and asked them if our schoolmaster came there every afternoon, but they said they had never seen any such fellow.'

41. Joshu's Zen

Joshu began the study of Zen when he was sixty years old and continued until he was eighty, when he realized Zen.

He taught from the age of eighty until he was one hundred and twenty.

A student once asked him: "If I haven't anything in my mind, what shall I do?"

Joshu replied: "Throw it out."

"But if I haven't anything, how can I throw it out?" continued the questioner.

"Well," said Joshu, "then carry it out."

42. The Dead Man's Answer

When Mamiya, who later became a well-known preacher, went to a teacher for personal guidance, he was asked to explain the sound of one hand.

Mamiya concentrated upon what the sound of one hand might be. "You are not working hard enough," his teacher told him. "You are too attached to food, wealth, things, and that sound. It would be better if you died. That would solve the problem."

The next time Mamiya appeared before his teacher he was again asked what he had to show regarding the sound of one hand. Mamiya at once fell over as if he were dead.

"You are dead all right," observed the teacher. "But how about that sound?"

"I haven't solved that yet," replied Mamiya, looking up.

"Dead men do not speak," said the teacher. "Get out!"

43. Zen in a Beggar's Life

Tosui was a well-known Zen teacher of his time. He had lived in several temples and taught in various provinces.

The last temple he visited accumulated so many adherents that Tosui told them he was going to quit the lecture business entirely. He advised them to disperse and go wherever they desired. After that no one could find any trace of him.

Three years later one of his disciples discovered him living with some beggars under a bridge in Kyoto. He at once implored Tosui to teach him.

"If you can do as I do for even a couple days, I might," Tosui replied.

So the former disciple dressed as a beggar and spent the day with Tosui. The following day one of the beggars died. Tosui and his pupil carried the body off at midnight and buried it on a mountainside. After that they returned to their shelter under the bridge.

Tosui slept soundly the remainder of the night, but the disciple could not sleep. When morning came Tosui said: "We do not have to beg food today. Our dead friend has left some over there." But the disciple was unable to eat a single bite of it.

"I have said you could not do as I," concluded Tosui. "Get out of here and do not bother me again."

44. The Thief Who Became a Disciple

One evening as Shichiri Kojun was reciting sutras a thief with a sharp sword entered, demanding either money or his life.

Shichiri told him: "Do not disturb me. You can find the money in that drawer." Then he resumed his recitation.

A little while afterwards he stopped and called: "Don't take it all. I need some to pay taxes with tomorrow."

The intruder gathered up most of the money and started to leave. "Thank a person when you receive a gift," Shichiri added. The man thanked him and made off.

A few days afterwards the fellow was caught and confessed, among others, the offence against Shichiri. When Shichiri was called as a witness he said: "This man is no thief, at least as far as I am concerned. I gave him money and he thanked me for it."

After he had finished his prison term, the man went to Shichiri and became his disciple.

45. Right and Wrong

When Bankei held his seclusion-weeks of meditation, pupils from many parts of Japan came to attend. During one of these gatherings a pupil was caught stealing. The matter was reported to Bankei with the request that the culprit be expelled. Bankei ignored the case.

Later the pupil was caught in a similar act, and again Bankei disregarded the matter. This angered the other pupils, who drew up a petition asking for the dismissal of the thief, stating that otherwise they would leave in a body.

When Bankei had read the petition he called everyone before him. "You are wise brothers," he told them. "You know what is right and what is not right. You may go somewhere else to study if you wish, but this poor brother does not even know right from wrong. Who will teach him if I do not? I am going to keep him here even if all the rest of you leave."

A torrent of tears cleansed the face of the brother who had stolen. All desire to steal had vanished.

46. How Grass and Trees Become Enlightened

During the Kamakura period, Shinkan studied Tendai six years and then studied Zen seven years; then he went to China and contemplated Zen for thirteen years more.

When he returned to Japan many desired to interview him and asked obscure questions. But when Shinkan received visitors, which was infrequently, he seldom answered their questions.

One day a fifty-year-old student of enlightenment said to Shinkan: "I have studied the Tendai school of thought since I was a little boy, but one thing in it I cannot understand. Tendai claims that even the grass and trees will become enlightened. To me this seems very strange."

"Of what use is it to discuss how grass and trees become enlightened?" asked Shinkan. "The question is how you yourself can become so. Did you even consider that?"

"I never thought of it that way," marveled the old man.

"Then go home and think it over," finished Shinkan.

47. *The Stingy Artist*

Gessen was an artist monk. Before he would start a drawing or painting he always insisted upon being paid in advance, and his fees were high. He was known as the "Stingy Artist."

A geisha once gave him a commission for a painting. "How much can you pay?" inquired Gessen.

"'Whatever you charge," replied the girl, "but I want you to do the work in front of me."

So on a certain day Gessen was called by the geisha. She was holding a feast for her patron.

Gessen with fine brush work did the paining. When it was completed he asked the highest sum of his time.

He received his pay. Then the geisha turned to her patron saying: "All this artist wants is money. His paintings are fine but his mind is dirty; money has caused it to become muddy. Drawn by such a filthy mind, his work is not fit to exhibit. It is just about good enough for one of my petticoats."

Removing her skirt, she then asked Gessen to do another picture on the back of her petticoat.

"How much will you pay?" asked Gessen.

"Oh, any amount," answered the girl.

Gessen named a fancy price, painted the picture in the manner requested, and went away.

It was learned later that Gessen had these reasons for desiring money:

A ravaging famine often visited his province. The rich would not help the poor, so Gessen had a secret warehouse, unknown to anyone, which he kept filled with grain, prepared for these emergencies.

From his village to the National Shrine the road was in very poor condition and many travelers suffered while traversing it. He desired to build a better road.

His teacher had passed away without realizing his wish to build a temple, and Gessen wished to complete this temple for him.

After Gessen had accomplished his three wishes he threw away his brushes and artist's materials and, retiring to the mountains, never painted again.

48. Accurate Proportion

Sen no Rikyu, a tea-master, wished to hang a flower basket on a column. He asked a carpenter to help him, directing the man to place it a little higher or lower, to the right or left, until he had found exactly the right spot. "That's the place," said Sen no Rikya finally.

The carpenter, to test the master, marked the spot and then pretended he had forgotten. Was this the place? "Was this the place, perhaps?" the carpenter kept asking, pointing to various places on the column.

But so accurate was the tea-master's sense of proportion that it was not until the carpenter reached the identical spot again that its location was approved.

49. Black-Nosed Buddha

A nun who was searching for enlightenment made a statue of Buddha and covered it with gold leaf. Wherever she ent she carried this golden Buddha with her.

Years passed and, still carrying her Buddha, the nun came to live in a small temple in a country where there were many Buddhas, each one with its own particular shrine.

The nun wished to burn incense before her golden Buddha. Not liking the idea of the perfume straying to others, she devised a funnel through which the smoke would ascend only to her statue. This blackened the nose of the golden Buddha, making it especially ugly.

50. Ryonen's Clear Realization

The Buddhist nun known as Ryonen was born in 1797. She was a graddaughter of the famous Japanese warrior Shingen. Her poetical genius and alluring beauty were such that at seventeen she was serving the empress as one of the ladies of the court. Even at such a youthful age fame awaited her.

The beloved empress died suddenly and Ryonen's hopeful dreams vanished. She became acutely aware of the impermanency of life in this world. It was then that she desired to study Zen.

Her relatives disagreed, however, and practically forced her into marriage. With a promise that she might become a nun aftr she had borne three children, Ryonen assented. Before she was twenty-five she had accomplished this condition. Then her husband and relatives could no longer dissuade her from her desire. She shaved her head, took the name of Ryonen, which means to realize clearly, and started on her pilgrimage.

She came to the city of Edo and asked Tetsugya to accept her as a disciple. At one glance the master rejected her because she was too beautiful.

Ryonen went to another master, Hakuo. Hakuo refused her for the same reason, saying that her beauty would only make trouble.

Ryonen obtained a hot iron and placed it against her face. In a few moments her beauty had vanished forever.

Hakuo then accepted her as a disciple.

Commemorating this occasion, Ryonen wrote a poem on the back of a little mirror:

In the service of my Empress I burned incense to perfume my exquisite clothes,

Now as a homeless mendicant I burn my face to enter a Zen temple.

When Ryonen was about to pass from this world, she wrote another poem:

Sixty-six times have these eyes beheld the changing scene of autumn.

I have said enough about moonlight,

Ask no more.

Only listen to the voice of pines and cedars when no wind stirs.

CHAPTER THREE

ZEN STORIES: 51-100

51. Sour Miso

The cook monk Dairyo, at Bankei's monastery, decided that he would take good care of his old teacher's health and give him only fresh miso, a paste of soy beans mixed with wheat and yeast that often ferments. Bankei, noticing that he was being served better miso than his pupils, asked: "Who is the cook today?"

Dairyo was sent before him. Bankei learned that according to his age and position he should eat only fresh miso. So he said to the cook: "Then you think I shouldn't eat at all." With this he entered his room and locked the door.

Dairyo, sitting outside the door, asked his teacher's pardon. Bankei would not answer. For seven days Dairyo sat outside and Bankei within.

Finally in desperation an adherent called loudly to Bankei: "You may be all right, old teacher, but this young disciple here has to eat. He cannot go without food forever!"

At that Bankei opened the door. He was smiling. He told Dairyo: "I insist on eating the same food as the least of my followers. Whe you become the teacher I do not want you to forget this."

52. Your Light May Go Out

A student of Tendai, a philosophical school of Buddhism, came to the Zen abode of Gasan as a pupil. When he was departing a few years later, Gasan warned him: "Studying the truth speculatively is useful as a way of collecting preaching material. But remember that unless you meditate constantly you light of truth may go out."

53. The Giver Should Be Thankful

While Seietsu was the master of Engaku in Kamakura he required larger quarters, since those in which he was teaching were overcrowded. Umeza Seibei a merchant of Edo, decided to donate five hundred pieces of gold called ryo toward the construction of a more commodious school. This money he brought to the teacher.

Seisetsu said: "All right. I will take it."

Umezu gave Seisetsu the sack of gold, but he was dissatisfied with the attitude of the teacher. One might live a whole year on three ryo, and the merchant had not even been thanked for five hundred.

"In that sack are five hundred ryo," hinted Umeza.

"You told me that before," replied Seisetsu.

"Even if I am a wealthy merchant, five hundred ryo is a lot of money," said Umezu.

"Do you want me to thank you for it?" asked Seisetsi.

"You ought to," replied Umeza.

"Why should I?" inquired Seisetsu. "The giver should be thankful."

54. The Last Will and Testament

Ikkyu, a famous Zen teacher of the Ashikaga era, was the son of the emperor. When he was very young, his mother left the palace and went to study Zen in a temple. In this way Prince Ikkyu also became a student. When this mother passed on, she left him a letter. It read:

To Ikkyu:

I have finished my work in this life and am now returning into Eternity. I wish you to become a good student and to realize your Buddha-nature. You will know if I am in hell and whether I am always with you or not.

If you become a man who realizes that the Buddha and his follower Bodhidharma are your own servants, you may leave off studying and work for humanity. The Buddha preached for forty-nine years and in all that time found it not necessary to speak one word. You ought to know why. But if you don't and yet wish to, avoid thinking fruitlessly.

Your Mother,
Not born, not dead.

September first.

P.S. The teaching of Buddha was mainly for the purpose of enlightening others. If you are dependent on any of its methods, you are naught but an ignorant insect. There are 80,000 books on Buddhism and if you should read all of them and still not see your own nature, you will not understand even this letter. This is my will and testament.

55. The Tea-Master and The Assassin

Taiko, a warrior who lived in Japan before the Tokugawa era, studied Cha-no-yu, tea etiquette, with Sen no Rikyu, a teacher of that aesthetical expression of calmness and contentment.

Taiko's attendant warrior Kato interpreted his superior's enthusiasm for tea etiquette as negligence of state affairs, so he decided to kill Sen no Rikyu. He pretended to make a social call upon the tea-master and was invited to drink tea.

The master, who was well skilled in his art, saw at a glance the warrior's intention, so he invited Kato to leave his sword outside before entering the room for the ceremony, explaining that Cha-no-yu represents peacefulness itself.

Kato would not listen to this. "I am a warrior," he said. "I always have my sword with me. Cha-no-yu or no Cha-no-yu, I have my sword."

"Very well. Bring your sword in and have some tea," consented Sen no Rikyu.

The kettle was boiling on the charcoal fire. Suddenly Sen no Rikyu tipped it over. Hissing steam arose, filling the room with smoke and ashes. The startled warrior ran outside.

The tea-master apologized. "It was my mistake. Come back in and have some tea. I have your sword here covered with ashes and will clean it and give it to you."

In this predicament the warrior realized he could not very well kill the tea-master, so he gave up the idea.

56. The True Path

Just before Ninakawa passed away the Zen master Ikkyu visited him. "Shall I lead you on?" Ikkyu asked.

Ninakawa replied: "I came here alone and I go alone. What help could you be to me?"

Ikkyu answered: "If you think you really come and go, that is your delusion. Let me show you the path on which there is no coming and going."

With his words, Ikkyu had revealed the path so clearly that Ninakawa smiled and passed away.

57. The Gates of Paradise

A soldier named Nobushige came to Hakuin, and asked: "Is there really a paradise and a hell?"

"Who are you?" inquired Hakuin.

"I am a samurai," the warrior replied.

"You, a soldier!" exclaimed Hakuin. "What kind of ruler would have you as his guard? Your face looks like that of a beggar."

Nobushige became so angry that he began to draw his sword, but Hakuin continued: "So you have a sword! Your weapon is probably much too dull to cut off my head."

As Nobushige drew his sword Hakuin remarked: "Here open the gates of hell!"

At these words the samurai, perceiving the master's discipline, sheathed his sword and bowed.

"Here open the gates of paradise," said Hakuin.

58. Arresting the Stone Buddha

A merchant bearing fifty rolls of cotton goods on his shoulders stopped to rest from the heat of the day beneath a shelter where a large stone Buddha was standing. There he fell asleep, and when he awoke his goods had disappeared. He immediately reported the matter to the police.

A judge named O-oka opened court to investigate. "That stone Buddha must have stolen the goods," concluded the judge. "He is supposed to care for the welfare of the people, but he has failed to perform his holy duty. Arrest him."

The police arrested the stone Buddha and carried it into the court. A noisy crowd followed the statue, curious to learn what kind of sentence the judge was about to impose.

When O-oka appeared on the bench he rebuked the boisterous audience. "What right have you people to appear before the court laughing and joking in this manner? You are in contempt of court and subject to a fine and imprisonment."

The people hastened to apologize. "I shall have to impose a fine on you," said the judge, "but I will remit it provided each one of you brings one roll of cotton goods to the court within three days. Anyone failing to do this will be arrested."

One of the rolls of cloth which the people brought was quickly recognized by the merchant as his own, and thus the thief was easily discovered. The merchant recovered his goods, and the cotton rolls were returned to the people.

59. Soldiers of Humanity

Once a division of the Japanese army was engaged in a sham battle, and some of the officers found it necessary to make their headquarters in Gasan's temple.

Gasan told his cook: "Let the officers have only the same simple fare we eat."

This made the army men angry, as they wre used to very deferential treatment. One came to Gasan and said: "Who do you think we are? We are soldiers, sacrificing our lives for our country. Why don't you treat us accordingly?"

Gasan answered sternly: "Who do you think we are? We are soldiers of humanity, aiming to save all sentient beings."

60. The Tunnel

Zenkai, the son of a samurai, journeyed to Edo and there became the retainer of a high official. He fell in love with the official's wife and was discovered. In self-defence, he slew the official. Then he ran away with the wife.

Both of them later became thieves. But the woman was so greedy that Zenkai grew disgusted. Finally, leaving her, he journeyed far away to the province of Buzen, where he became a wandering mendicant.

To atone for his past, Zenkai resolved to accomplish some good deed in his lifetime. Knowing of a dangerous road over a cliff that had caused death and injury to many persons, he resolved to cut a tunnel through the mountain there.

Begging food in the daytime, Zenkai worked at night digging his tunnel. When thirty years had gone by, the tunnel was 2,280 feet long, 20 feet high, and 30 feet wide.

Two years before the work was completed, the son of the official he had slain, who was a skillful swordsman, found Zenkai out and came to kill him in revenge.

"I will gived you my life willingly," said Zenkai. "Only let me finish this work. On the day it is completed, then you may kill me."

So the son awaited the day. Several months passed and Zenkai kept digging. The son grew tired of doing nothing and began to help with the digging. After he had helped for more than a year, he came to admire Zenkai's strong will and character.

At last the tunnel was completed and the people could use it and travel safely.

"Now cut off my head," said Zenkai. "My work is done."

"How can I cut off my own teacher's head?" asked the younger man with tears in his eyes.

61. Gudo and the Emperor

The emperor Goyozei was studying Zen under Gudo. He inquired: "In Zen this very mind is Buddha. Is this correct?"

Gudo answered: "If I say yes, you will think that you understand without understanding. If I say no, I would be contradicting a fact which you may understand quite well."

On another day the emperor asked Gudo: "Where does the enlightened man go when he dies?"

Gudo answered: "I know not."

"Why don't you know?" asked the emperor.

"Because I have not died yet," replied Gudo.

The emperor hesitated to inquire further about these things his mind could not grasp. So Gudo beat the floor with his hand as if to awaken him, and the emperor was enlightened!

The emperor respected Zen and old Gudo more than ever after his enlightenment, and he even permitted Gudo to wear his hat in the palace in winter. When Gudo was over eighty he used to fall asleep in the midst of his lecture, and the emperor would quietly retire to another room so his beloved teacher might enjoy the rest his aging body required.

62. *In the Hands of Destiny*

A great Japanese warrior named Nobunaga decided to attack the enemy although he had only one-tenth the number of men the opposition commanded. He knew that he would win, but his soldiers were in doubt.

On the way he stopped at a Shinto shrine and told his men: "After I visit the shrine I will toss a coin. If heads comes, we will win; if tails, we will lose. Destiny holds us in her hand."

Nobunaga entered the shrine and offered a silent prayer. He came forth and tossed a coin. Heads appeared. His soldiers were so eager to fight that they won their battle easily.

"No one can change the hand of destiny," his attendant told him after the battle.

"Indeed not," said Nobunaga, showing a coin which had been doubled, with heads facing either way.

63. *Killing*

Gasan instructed his adherents one day: "Those who speak against killing and who desire to spare the lives of all conscious beings are right. It is good to protect even animals and insects. But what about those persons who kill time, what about those who are destroying wealth, and those who destroy political economy? We should not overlook them. Furthermore, what of the one who preaches without enlightenment? He is killing Buddhism."

64. *Kasan Sweat*

Kasan was asked to officiate at the funeral of a provincial lord.

He had never met lords and nobles before so he was nervous. When the ceremony started, Kasan sweat.

Afterwards, when he had returned, he gathered his pupils together. Kasan confessed that he was not yet qualified to be a teacher for he lacked the sameness of bearing in the world of fame that he possessed in the secluded temple. Then Kasan resigned and became a pupil of another master. Eight years later he returned to his former pupils, enlightened.

65. *The Subjugation of a Ghost*

A young wife fell sick and was about to die. "I love you so much," she told her husband, "I do not want to leave you. Do not go from me to any other woman. If you do, I will return as a ghost and cause you endless trouble."

Soon the wife passed away. The husband respected her last wish for the first three months, but then he met another woman and fell in love with her. They became engaged to be married.

Immediately after the engagement a ghost appeared every night to the man, blaming him for not keeping his promise. The ghost was clever too. She told him exactly what has transpired between himself and his new sweetheart. Whenever he gave his fiancee a present, the ghost would describe it in detail. She would even repeat conversations, and it so annoyed the man that he could not sleep. Someone advised him to take his problem to a Zen master who lived close to the village. At length, in despair, the poor man went to him for help.

"Your former wife became a ghost and knows everything you do," commented the master. "Whatever you do or say, whatever you give you beloved, she knows. She must be a very wise ghost. Really you should admire such a ghost. The next time she appears, bargain with her. Tell her that she knows so much you can hide nothing from her, and that if she will answer you one question, you promise to break your engagement and remain single."

"What is the question I must ask her?" inquired the man.

The master replied: "Take a large handful of soy beans and ask her exactly how many beans you hold in your hand. If she cannot tell you, you will know she is only a figment of your imagination and will trouble you no longer."

The next night, when the ghost appeared the man flattered her and told her that she knew everything.

"Indeed," replied the ghost, "and I know you went to see that Zen master today."

"And since you know so much," demanded the man, "tell me how many beans I hold in this hand!"

There was no longer any ghost to answer the question.

66. Children of His Majesty

Yamaoka Tesshu was a tutor of the emperor. He was also a master of fencing and a profound student of Zen.

His home was the abode of vagabonds. He has but one suit of clothes, for they kept him always poor.

The emperor, observing how worn his garments were, gave Yamaoka some money to buy new ones. The next time Yamaoka appeared he wore the same old outfit.

"What became of the new clothes, Yamaoka?" asked the emperor.

"I provided clothes for the children of Your Majesty," explained Yamaoka.

67. What Are You Doing! What Are You Saying!

In modern times a great deal of nonsense is talked about masters and disciples, and about the inheritance of a master's teaching by favorite pupils, entitling them to pass the truth on to their adherents. Of course Zen should be imparted in this way, from heart to heart, and in the past it was really accomplished. Silence and humility reigned rather than profession and assertion. The one who received such a teaching kept the matter hidden even after twenty years. Not until another discovered through his own need that a real master was at hand was it learned that the teching had been imparted, and even then the occasion arose quite naturally and the teaching made its way in its own right. Under no circumstance did the teacher even claim "I am the successor of So-and-so." Such a claim would prove quite the contrary.

The Zen master Mu-nan had only one successor. His name was Shoju. After Shoju had completed his study of Zen, Mu-nan called him into his room. "I am getting old," he said, "and as far as I know, Shoju, you are the only one who will carry on this teaching. Here is a book. It has been passed down from master to master for seven generations. I have also added many points according to my understanding. The book is very valuable, and I am giving it to you to represent your successorhip."

"If the book is such an important thing, you had better keep it," Shoju replied. "I received your Zen without writing and am satisfied with it as it is."

"I know that," said Mu-nan. "Even so, this work has been carried from master to master for seven generations, so you may keep it as a symbol of having received the teaching. Here."

They happened to be talking before a brazier. The instant Shoju felt the book in his hands he thrust it into the flaming coals. He had no lust for possessions.

Mu-nan, who never had been angry before, yelled: "What are you doing!"

Shoju shouted back: "What are you saying!"

68. *One Note of Zen*

After Kakua visited the emperor he disappeared and no one knew what became of him. He was the first Japanese to study Zen in China, but since he showed nothing of it, save one note, he is not remembered for having brought Zen into his country.

Kakua visited China and accepted the true teaching. He did not travel while he was there. Meditating constantly, he lived on a remote part of a mountain. Whenever people found him and asked him to preach he would say a few words and then move to another part of the mountain where he could be found less easily.

The emperor heard about Kakua when he returned to Japan and asked him to preach Zen for his edification and that of his subjects.

Kakua stood before the emperor in silence. He the produced a flute from the folds of his robe, and blew one short note. Bowing politely, he disappeared.

69. *Eating the Blame*

Circumstances arose one day which delayed preperation of the dinner of a Soto Zen master, Fukai, and his followers. In haste the cook went to the garden with his curved knife and cut off the tops of green vegetables, chopped them together and made soup, unaware that in his haste he had included a part of a snake in the vegetables.

The followers of Fugai thought they never tasted such good soup. But when the master himself found the snake's head in his bowl, he summoned the cook. "What is this?" he demanded, holding yo the head of the snake.

"Oh, thank you, master," replied the cook, taking the morsel and eating it quickly.

70. The Most Valuable Thing in the World

Sozan, a Chinese Zen master, was asked by a student: "What is the most valuable thing in the world?"

The master replied: "The head of a dead cat."

"Why is the head of a dead cat the most valuable thing in the world?" inquired the student.

Sozan replied: "Because no one can name its price."

71. Learning to Be Silent

The pupils of the Tendai school used to study meditation before Zen entered Japan. Four of them who were intimate friends promised one another to observe seven days of silence.

On the first day all were silent. Their meditation had begun auspiciously, but when night came and the oil lamps were growing dim one of the pupils could not help exclaiming to a servant: "Fix those lamps."

The second pupils was surprised to hear the first one talk. "We are not supposed to say a word," he remarked.

"You two are stupid. Why did you talk?" asked the third.

"I am the only one who has not talked," concluded the fourth pupil.

72. The Blockhead Lord

Two Zen teachers, Daigu and Gudo, were invited to visit a lord. Upon arriving, Gudo said to the lord: "You are wise by nature and have an inborn ability to learn Zen."

"Nonsense," said Daigu. "Why do you flatter this blockhead? He may be a lord, but he doesn't know anything of Zen."

So, instead of building a temple for Gudo, the lord built it for Daigu and studied Zen with him.

73. Ten Successors

Zen pupils take a vow that even if they are killed by their teacher, they intend to learn Zen. Usually they cut a finger and seal their resolution with blood. In time the vow has become a mere formality, and for this reason the pupil who died by the hand of Ekido was made to appear a martyr.

Ekido had become a severe teacher. His pupils feared him. One of them on duty, striking the gong to tell the time of day, missed his beats when his eye was attracted by a beautiful girl passing the temple gate.

At that moment Ekido, who was directly behind him, hit him with a stick and the shock happened to kill him.

The pupil's guardian, hearing of the accident, went directly to Ekido. Knowing that he was not to blame he praised the master for his severe teaching. Ekido's attitude was just the same as if the pupil were still alive.

After this took place, he was able to produce under his guidance more than ten enlightened successors, a very unusual number.

74. *True Reformation*

Ryokan devoted his life to the study of Zen. One day he heard that his nephew, despite the admonitions of relatives, was spending his money on a courtesan. Inasmuch as the nephew had taken Ryokan's place in managing the family estate and the property was in danger of being dissipated, the relatives asked Ryoken to do something about it.

Ryokan had to travel a long way to visit his nephew, whom he had not seen for many years. The nephew seemed pleased to meet his uncle again and invited him to remain overnight.

All night Ryokan sat in meditation. As he was departing in the morning he said to the young man: "I must be getting old, my hand shakes so. Will you help me tie the string of my straw sandal?"

The nephew helped him willingly. "Thank you," finished Ryokan, "you see, a man becomes older and feebler day by day. Take good care of yourself." Then Ryokan left, never mentioning a word about the courtesan or the complaints of the relatives. But, from that morning on, the dissipations of the nephew ended

75. *Temper*

A Zen student came to Bankei and complained: "Master, I have an ungovernable temper. How can I cure it?"

"You have something very strange," replied Bankei. "Let me see what you have."

"Just now I cannot show it to you," replied the other.

"When can you show it to me?" asked Bankei.

"It arises unexpectedly," replied the student.

"Then," concluded Bankei, "it must not be your own true nature. If it were, you could show it to me at any time. When you were born you did not have it, and your parents did not give it to you. Think that over."

76. The Stone Mind

Hogen, a Chinese Zen teacher, lived alone in a small temple in the country. One day four traveling monks appeared and asked if they might make a fire in his yard to warm themselves.

While they were building the fire, Hogen heard them arguing about subjectivity and objectivity. He joined them and said: "There is a big stone. Do you consider it to be inside or outside your mind?"

One of the monks replied: "From the Buddhist viewpoint everything is an objectification of mind, so I would say that the stone is inside my mind."

"Your head must feel very heavy," observed Hogen, "if you are carrying around a stone like that in your mind."

77. No Attachment to Dust

Zengetsu, a Chinese master of the T'ang dynasty, wrote the following advice for his pupils:

Living in the world yet not forming attachments to the dust of the world is the way of a true Zen student.

When witnessing the good action of another encourage yourself to follow his example. Hearing of the mistaken action of another, advise yourself not to emulate it.

Even though alone in a dark room, be as if you were facing a noble guest. Express your feelings, but become no more expressive than your true nature.

Poverty is your treasure. Never exchange it for an easy life.

A person may appear a fool and yet not be one. He may only be guarding his wisdom carefully.

Virtues are the fruit of self-discipline and do not drop from heaven of themselves as does rain or snow.

Modesty is the foundation of all virtues. Let your neighbors discover you before you make yourself known to them.

A noble heart never forces itself forward. Its words are as rare gems, seldom displayed and of great value.

To a sincere student, every day is a fortunate day. Time passes but he never lags behind. Neither glory nor shame can move him.

Censure yourself, never another. Do not discuss right and wrong.

Some things, though right, were considered wrong for generations. Since the value of righteousness may be recognized after centuries, there is no need to crave immediate appreciation.

Live with cause and leave results to the great law of the universe. Pass each day in peaceful contemplation.

78. Real Prosperity

A rich man asked Sengai to write something for the continued prosperity of his family so that it might be treasured from generation to generation.

Sengai obtained a large sheet of paper and wrote: "Father dies, son dies, grandson dies."

The rich man became angry. "I asked you to write something for the happiness of my family! Why do you make such a joke of this?"

"No joke is intended," explained Sengai. "If before you yourself die your son should die, this would grieve you greatly. If your grandson should pass away before your son, both of you would be broken-hearted. If your family, generation after generation, passes away in the order I have named, it will be the natural course of life. I call this real prosperity."

79. Incense Burner

A woman of Nagasaki named Kame was one of the few makers of incense burners in Japan. Such a burner is a work of art to be used only in a tearoom of before a family shrine.

Kame, whose father before her had been such an artist, was fond of drinking. She also smoked and associated with men most of the time. Whenever she made a little money she gave a feast inviting artists, poets, carpenters, workers, men of many vocations and avocations. In their association she evolved her designs.

Kame was exceedingly slow in creating, but when her work was finished it was always a masterpiece. Her burners were treasured in homes whose womanfolk never drank, smoked, or associated freely with men.

The mayor of Nagasaki once requested Kame to design an incense burner for him. She delayed doing so until almost half a year had passed. At that time the mayor, who had been promoted to office in a distant city, visited her. He urged Kame to begin work on his burner.

At last receiving the inspiration, Kame made the incense burner. After it was completed she placed it upon a table. She looked at it long and carefully. She smoked and drank before it as if it were her own company. All day she observed it.

At last, picking up a hammer, Kame smashed it to bits. She saw it was not the perfect creation her mind demanded.

80. The Real Miracle

When Bankei was preaching at Ryumon temple, a Shinshu priest, who believed in salvation through repetition of the name of the Buddha of Love, was jealous of his large audience and wanted to debate with him.

Bankei was in the midst of a talk when the priest appeared, but the fellow made such a disturbance that Bankei stopped his discourse and asked about the noise.

"The founder of our sect," boasted the priest, "had such miraculous powers that he held a brush in his hand on one bank of the river, his attendant held up a paper on the other bank, and the teacher wrote the holy name of Amida through the air. Can you do such a wonderful thing?"

Bankei replied lightly: "Perhaps your fox can perform that trick, but that is not the manner of Zen. My miracle is that when I feel hungry I eat, and when I feel thirsty I drink."

81. Just Go to Sleep

Gasan was sitting at the bedside of Tekisui three days before his teacher's passing. Tekisui had already chosen him as his successor.

A temple recently had burned and Gasan was busy rebuilding the structure. Tekisui asked him: "What are you going to do when you get the temple rebuilt?"

"When your sickness is over we want you to speak there," said Gasan.

"Suppose I do not live until then?"

"Then we will get someone else," replied Gasan.

"Suppose you cannot find anyone?" continued Tekisui.

Gasan answered loudly: "Don't ask such foolish questions. Just go to sleep."

82. *Nothing Exists*

Yamaoka Tesshu, as a young student of Zen, visited one master after another. He called upon Dokuon of Shokoku.

Desiring to show his attainment, he said: "The mind, Buddha, and sentient beings, after all, do not exist. The true nature of phenomena is emptiness. There is no realization, no delusion, no sage, no mediocrity. There is no giving and nothing to be received."

Dokuon, who was smoking quietly, said nothing. Suddenly he whacked Yamaoka with his bamboo pipe. This made the youth quite angry.

"If nothing exists," inquired Dokuon, "where did this anger come from?"

83. *No Work, No Food*

Hyakujo, the Chinese Zen master, used to labor with his pupils even at the age of eighty, trimming the gardens, cleaning the grounds, and pruning the trees.

The pupils felt sorry to see the old teacher working so hard, but they knew he would not listen to their advice to stop, so they hid away his tools.

That day the master did not eat. The next day he did not eat, nor the next. "He may be angry because we have hidden his tools," the pupils surmised. "We had better put them back."

The day they did, the teacher worked and ate the same as before. In the evening he instructed them: "No work, no food."

84. *True Friends*

A long time ago in China there were two friends, one who played the harp skilfully and one who listen skillfully.

When the one played or sang about a mountain, the other would say: "I can see the mountain before us."

When the one played about water, the listener would exclaim: "Here is the running stream!"

But the listener fell sick and died. The first friend cut the strings of his harp and never played again. Since that time the cutting of harp strings has always been a sign of intimate friendship.

85. Time to Die

Ikkyu, the Zen master, was very clever even as a boy. His teacher had a precious teacup, a rare antique. Ikkyu happened to break this cup and was greatly perplexed. Hearing the footsteps of his teacher, he held the pieces of the cup behind him. When the master appeared, Ikkyu asked: "Why do people have to die?"

"This is natural," explained the older man. "Everything has to die and has just so long to live."

Ikkyu, producing the shattered cup, added: "It was time for your cup to die."

86. The Living Buddha and the Tubmaker

Zen masters give personal guidance in a secluded room. No one enters while teacher and pupil are together.

Mokurai, the Zen master of Kennin temple in Kyoto, used to enjoy talking with merchants and newspapermen as well as with his pupils. A certain tubmaker was almost illiterate. He would ask foolish questions of Mokurai, have tea, and then go away.

One day while the tubmaker was there Mokurai wished to give personal guidance to a disciple, so he asked the tubmaker to wait in another room.

"I understand you are a living Buddha," the man protested. "Even the stone Buddhas in the temple never refuse the numerous persons who come together before them. Why then should I be excluded?"

Mokurai had to go outside to see his disciple.

87. Three Kinds of Disciples

A Zen master named Gettan lived in the latter part of the Tokugawa era. He used to say: "There are three kinds of disciples: those who impart Zen to others, those who maintain the temples and shrines, and then there are the rice bags and the clothes-hangers."

Gasan expressed the same idea. When he was studying under Tekisui, his teacher was very severe. Sometimes he even beat him. Other pupils would not stand this kind of teaching and quit. Gasan remained, saying:

"A poor disciple utilizes a teacher's influence. A fair disciple admires a teacher's kindness. A good disciple grows strong under a teacher's discipline."

88. *How to Write a Chinese Poem*

A well-known Japanese poet was asked how to compose a Chinese poem.

"The usual Chinese poem is four lines," he explains. "The first line contains the initial phase; the second line, the continuation of that phase; the third line turns from this subject and begins a new one; and the fourth line brings the first three lines together. A popular Japanese song illustrates this:

Two daughters of a silk merchant live in Kyoto.

The elder is twenty, the younger, eighteen.

A soldier may kill with his sword.

But these girls slay men with their eyes.

89. *Zen Dialogue*

Zen teachers train their young pupils to express themselves. Two Zen temples each had a child protégé. One child, going to obtain vegetables each morning, would meet the other on the way.

"Where are you going?" asked the one.

"I am going wherever my feet go," the other responded.

This reply puzzled the first child who went to his teacher for help. "Tomorrow morning," the teacher told him, "when you meet that little fellow, ask him the same question. He will give you the same answer, and then you ask him: 'Suppose you have no feet, then where are you going?' That will fix him."

The children met again the following morning.

"Where are you going?" asked the first child.

"I am going wherever the wind blows," answered the other.

This again nonplussed the youngster, who took his defeat to his teacher.

"Ask him where he is going if there is no wind," suggested the teacher.

The next day the children met a third time.

"Where are you going?" asked the first child.

"I am going to the market to buy vegetables," the other replied.

90. The Last Rap

Tangen had studied with Sengai since childhood. When he was twenty he wanted to leave his teacher and visit others for comparative study, but Sengai would not permit this. Every time Tangen suggested it, Sengai would give him a rap on the head.

Finally Tangen asked an elder brother to coax permission from Sengai. This the brother did and then reported to Tangen: "It is arranged. I have fixed it for you start your pilgrimage at once."

Tangen went to Sengai to thank him for his permission. The master answered by giving him another rap.

When Tangen related this to his elder brother the other said: "What is the matter? Sengai has no business giving permission and then changing his mind. I will tell him so." And off he went to see the teacher.

"I did not cancel my permission," said Sengai. "I just wished to give him one last smack over the head, for when he returns he will be enlightened and I will not be able to reprimand him again."

91. The Taste of Banzo's Sword

Matajuro Yagyu was the son of a famous swordsman. His father, believing that his son's work was too mediocre to anticipate mastership, disowned him.

So Matajuro went to Mount Futara and there found the famous swordsman Banzo. But Banzo confirmed the father's judgment. "You wish to learn swordsmanship under my guidance?" asked Banzo. "You cannot fulfill the requirements."

"But if I work hard, how many years will it take to become a master?" persisted the youth.

"The rest of your life," replied Banzo.

"I cannot wait that long," explained Matajuro. "I am willing to pass through any hardship if only you will teach me. If I become your devoted servant, how long might it be?"

"Oh, maybe ten years," Banzo relented.

"My father is getting old, and soon I must take care of him," continued Matajuro. "If I work far more intensively, how long would it take me?"

"Oh, maybe thirty years," said Banzo.

"Why is that?" asked Matajuro. "First you say ten and now thirty years. I will undergo any hardship to master this art in the shortest time!"

"Well," said Banzo, "in that case you will have to remain with me for seventy years. A man in such a hurry as you are to get results seldom learns quickly."

"Very well," declared the youth, understanding at last that he was being rebuked for impatience, "I agree."

Matajuro was told never to speak of fencing and never to touch a sword. He cooked for his master, washed the dishes, made his bed, cleaned the yard, cared for the garden, all without a word of swordmanship.

Three years passed. Still Matajuro labored on. Thinking of his future, he was sad. He had not even begun to learn the art to which he had devoted his life.

But one day Banzo crept up behind him and gave him a terrific blow with a wooden sword.

The following day, when Matajuro was cooking rice, Banzo again sprang upon him unexpectedly.

After that, day and night, Matajuro had to defend himself from unexpected thrusts. Not a moment passed in any day that he did not have to think of the taste of Banzo's sword.

He learned so rapidly he brought smiles to the face of his master. Matajuro became the greatest swordsman in the land.

92. Fire-Poker Zen

Hakuin used to tell his pupils about an old woman who had a teashop, praising her understanding of Zen. The pupils refused to believe what he told them and would go to the teashop to find out for themselves.

Whenever the woman saw them coming she could tell at once whether they had come for tea or to look into her grasp of Zen. In the former case, she would serve them graciously. In the latter, she would beckon the pupils to come behind her screen. The instant they obeyed, she would strike them with a fire-poker.

Nine out of ten of them could not escape her beating.

93. Storyteller's Zen

Encho was a famous storyteller. His tales of love stirred the hearts of his listeners. When he narrated a story of war, it was as if the listeners themselves were in the field of battle.

One day Encho met Yamaoka Tesshu, a layman who had almost embraced masterhood of Zen. "I understand," said Yamaoka, "you ar the best storyteller in out land and that you make people cry or laugh at will. Tell me my favorite story of the Peach Boy. When I was a little tot I used to sleep beside my mother, and she often related this legend. In the middle of the story I would fall asleep. Tell it to me just as my mother did."

Encho dared not attempt this. He requested time to study. Several months later he went to Yamaoka and said: "Please give me the opportunity to tell you the story."

"Some other day," answered Yamaoka.

Encho was keenly disappointed. He studied further and tried again. Yamaoka rejected him many times. When Encho would start to talk Yamaoka would stop him, saying: "You are not yet like my mother."

It took Encho five years to be able to tell Yamaoka the legend as his mother had told it to him.

In this way, Yamaoka imparted Zen to Encho.

94. Midnight Excursion

Many pupils were studying meditation under the Zen master Sengai. One of them used to arise at night, climb over the temple wall, and go to town on a pleasure jaunt.

Sengai, inspecting the dormitory quarters, found this pupil missing one night and also discovered the high stool he had used to scale the wall. Sengai removed the stool and stood there in its place.

When the wanderer returned, not knowing that Sengai was the stool, he put his feet on the master's head and jumped down into the grounds. Discovering what he had done, he was aghast.

Sengai said: "It is very chilly in the early morning. Do be careful not to catch cold yourself."

The pupil never went out at night again.

95. A Letter to a Dying Man

Bassui wrote the following letter to one of his disciples who was about to die:

"The essence of your mind is not born, so it will never die. It is not an existance, which is perishable. It is not an emptiness, which is a mere void. It has neither color nor form. It enjoys no pleasures and suffers no pains.

"I know you are very ill. Like a good Zen student, you are facing that sickness squarely. You may not know exactly who is suffering, but question yourself: What is the essence of this mind? Think only of this. You will need no more. Covet nothing. Your end which is endless is as a snowflake dissolving in the pure air."

96. *A Drop of Water*

A Zen master named Gisan asked a young student to bring him a pail of water to cool his bath.

The student brought the water and, after cooling the bath, threw on to the ground the little that was left over.

"You dunce!" the master scolded him. "Why didn't you give the rest of the water to the plants? What right have you to waste even one drop of water in this temple?"

The young student attained Zen in that instant. He changed his name to Tekisui, which means a drop of water.

97. *Teaching the Ultimate*

In early times in Japan, bamboo-and-paper lanterns were used with candles inside. A blind man, visiting a friend one night, was offered a lantern to carry home with him.

"I do not need a lantern," he said. "Darkness or light is all the same to me."

"I know you do not need a lantern to find your way," his friend replied, "but if you don't have one, someone else may run into you. So you must take it."

The blind man started off with the lantern and before he had walked very far someone ran squarely into him. "Look out where you are going!" he exclaimed to the stranger. "Can't you see this lantern?"

"Your candle has burned out, brother," replied the stranger.

98. Non-Attachment

Kitano Gempo, abbot of Eihei temple, was ninely-two years old when he passed away in the year 1933. He endeavored his whole life not to be attached to anything. As a wandering mendicant when he was twenty he happened to meet a traveler who smoked tobacco. As they walked together down a mountain road, they stopped under a tree to rest. The traveler offered Kitano a smoke, which he accepted, as he was very hungry at the time.

"How pleasant this smoking is," he commented. The other gave him an extra pipe and tobacco and they parted.

Kitano felt: "Such pleasant things may disturb meditation. Before this goes too far, I will stop now." So he threw the smoking outfit away.

When he was twenty-three years old he studied I-King, the profoundest doctrine of the universe. It was winter at the time and he needed some heavy clothes. He wrote his teacher, who lived a hundred miles away, telling him of his need, and gave the letter to a traveler to deliver. Almost the whole winter passed and neither answer nor clothes arrived. So Kitano resorted to the prescience of I-King, which also teaches the art of divination, to determine whether or not his letter had miscarried. He found that this had been the case. A letter afterwards from his teacher made no mention of clothes.

"If I perform such accurate determinative work with I-King, I may neglect my meditation," felt Kitano. So he gave up this marvelous teaching and never resorted to its powers again.

When he was twenty-eight he studied Chinese calligraphy and poetry. He grew so skillful in these arts that his teacher praised him. Kitano mused: "If I don't stop now, I'll be a poet, not a Zen teacher." So he never wrote another poem.

99. Tosui's Vinegar

Tosui was the Zen master who left the formalism of temples to live under a bridge with beggars. When he was getting very old, a friend helped him to earn his living without begging. He showed Tosui how to collect rice and manufacture vinegar from it, and Tosui did this until he passed away.

While Tosui was making vinegar, one of the beggars gave him a picture of the Buddha. Tosui hung it on the wall of his hut and put a sign beside it.

The sign read:

Mr. Amida Buddha: This little room is quite narrow. I can let you remain as a transient. But don't think I am asking you to be reborn in your paradise.

100. The Silent Temple

Shoichi was a one-eyed teacher of Zen, sparkling with enlightenment. He taught his disciples in Tofuku temple.

Day and night the whole temple stood in silence. There was no sound at all.

Even the reciting of sutras was abolished by the teacher. His pupils had nothing to do but meditate.

When the master passed away, an old neighbor heard the ringing of bells and the recitation of sutras. Then she knew Shoichi had gone.

101. Buddha's Zen

Buddha said: "I consider the positions of kings and rulers as that of dust motes. I observe treasures of gold and gems as so many bricks and pebbles. I look upon the finest silken robes as tattered rags. I see myriad worlds of the universe as small seeds of fruit, and the greatest lake in India as a drop of oil on my foot. I perceive the teachings of the world to be the illusion of magicians. I discern the highest conception of emancipation as a golden brocade in a dream, and view the holy path of the illuminated ones as flowers appearing in one's eyes. I see meditation as a pillar of a mountain, Nirvana as a nightmare of daytime. I look upon the judgment of right and wrong as the serpentine dance of a dragon, and the rise and fall of beliefs as but traces left by the four seasons."

CHAPTER FOUR

CONCENTRATION

1. Concentration

After winning several archery contests, the young and rather boastful champion challenged a Zenmaster who was renowned for his skill as an archer. The young man demonstrated remarkable technical proficiency when he hit a distant bull's eye on his first try, and then split that arrow with his second shot. "There," he said to the old man, "see if you can match that!" Undisturbed, the master did not draw his bow, but rather motioned for theyoung archer to follow him up the mountain. Curious about the old fellow's intentions, the champion followed him high into the mountain until they reached a deep chasm spanned by a rather flimsy and shaky log. Calmly stepping out onto the middle of the unsteady and certainly perilous bridge, the old master picked a far away tree as a target, drew his bow, and fired a clean, direct hit. "Now it is your turn," he said as he gracefully stepped back onto the safe ground. Staring with terror into the seemingly bottomless and beckoning abyss, the young man could not force himself to step out onto the log, no less shoot at a target. "You have much skill with your bow," the master said, sensing his challenger's predicament, "but you have little skill with the mind that lets loose the shot."

2. Destiny

During a momentous battle, a Japanese general decided to attack even though his army was greatly outnumbered. He was confident they would win, but his men were filled with doubt. On the way to the battle, they stopped at a religious shrine. After praying with the men, the general took out a coin and said, "I shall now toss this coin. If it is heads, we shall win. If tails, we shall lose. Destiny will now reveal itself."

He threw the coin into the air and all watched intently as it landed. It was heads. The soldiers were so overjoyed and filled with confidence that they vigorously attacked the enemy and were victorious. After the battle, a lieutenant remarked to the general, "No one can change destiny." "Quite right," the general replied as he showed the lieutenant the coin, which had heads on both sides.

3. Egotism

The Prime Minister of the Tang Dynasty was a national hero for his success as both a statesman and military leader. But despite his fame, power, and wealth, he considered himself a humble and devout Buddhist. Often he visited his favorite Zen master to study under him, and they seemed to get along very well. The fact that he was prime minister apparently had no effect on their relationship, which seemed to be simply one of a revered master and respectful student.

One day, during his usual visit, the Prime Minister asked the master, "Your Reverence, what is egotism according to Buddhism?" The master's face turned red, and in a very condescending and insulting tone of voice, he shot back, "What kind of stupid question is that!?" This unexpected response so shocked the Prime Minister that he became sullen and angry. The Zen master then smiled and said, "THIS, Your Excellency, is egotism."

4. Story of a Monk

A monk decides to meditate alone, away from his monastery. He takes his boat out to the middle of the lake, moors it there, closes his eyes and begins his meditation.

After a few hours of undisturbed silence, he suddenly feels the bump of another boat colliding with his own. With his eyes still closed, he senses his anger rising, and by the time he opens his eyes, he is ready to scream at the boatman who dared disturb his meditation.

But when he opens his eyes, he sees it's an empty boat that had probably got untethered and floated to the middle of the lake.

At that moment, the monk achieves self-realization, and understands that the anger is within him; it merely needs the bump of an external object to provoke it out of him.

From then on, whenever he comes across someone who irritates him or provokes him to anger, he reminds himself, "The other person is merely an empty boat. The anger is within me."

Some useful timeless tips

1. Throw out nonessential numbers. This includes age, weight and height. Let the doctors worry about them. That is why you pay 'them'

2. Keep only cheerful friends. The grouches pull you down.

3. Keep learning. Learn more about the computer, crafts, gardening, whatever. Never let the brain idle. 'An idle mind is the devil's workshop.' And the devil's name is Alzheimer's.

4. Enjoy the simple things.

5.. Laugh often, long and loud. Laugh until you gasp for breath.

6. The tears happen. Endure, grieve, and move on. The only person, who is with us our entire life, is ourselves. Be ALIVE while you are alive.

7. Surround yourself with what you love, whether it's family, pets, keepsakes, music, plants, hobbies, whatever. Your home is your refuge.

8. Cherish your health: If it is good, preserve it. If it is unstable, improve it. If it is beyond what you can improve, get help.

9. Don't take guilt trips. Take a trip to the mall, even to the next county; to a foreign country but NOT to where the guilt is.

10. Tell the people you love that you love them, at every opportunity.

AND ALWAYS REMEMBER: Life is not measured by the number of breaths we take, but by the moments that take our breath away.

We all need to live life to its fullest each day, Worry about nothing, pray about everything!!!

5. The Pointer

The Zen teacher's dog loved his evening romp with his master. The dog would bound ahead to fetch a stick, then run back, wag his tail, and wait for the next game. On this particular evening, the teacher invited one of his brightest students to join him – a boy so intelligent that he became troubled by the contradictions in Buddhist doctrine.

"You must understand," said the teacher, "that words are only guideposts. Never let the words or symbols get in the way of truth. Here, I'll show you."

With that the teacher called his happy dog.

"Fetch me the moon," he said to his dog and pointed to the full moon.

"Where is my dog looking?" asked the teacher of the bright pupil.

"He's looking at your finger."

"Exactly. Don't be like my dog. Don't confuse the pointing finger with the thing that is being pointed at. All our Buddhist words are only guideposts. Every man fights his way through other men's words to find his own truth."

6. *Flow Like a River*

There is the story of a young martial arts student who was under the tutelage of a famous master.

One day, the master was watching a practice session in the courtyard. He realized that the presence of the other students was interfering with the young man's attempts to perfect his technique.

The master could sense the young man's frustration. He went up to the young man and tapped him on his shoulder.

"What's the problem?" he inquired.

"I don't know", said the youth, with a strained expression.

"No matter how much I try, I am unable to execute the moves properly".

"Before you can master technique, you must understand harmony. Come with me, I will explain", replied the master.

The teacher and student left the building and walked some distance into the woods until they came upon a stream. The master stood silently on the bank for several moments. Then he spoke.

"Look at the stream," he said. "There are rocks in its way. Does it slam into them out of frustration? It simply flows over and around them and moves on! Be like the water and you will know what harmony is."

The young man took the master's advice to heart. Soon, he was barely noticing the other students around him. Nothing could come in his way of executing the most perfect moves.

7. *No Objective World*

Once there was a monk who specialized in the Buddhist precepts, and he kept to them all his life. Once when he was walking at night, he stepped on something. It made a squishing sound, and he imagined he had stepped on an egg-bearing frog.

This caused him no end of alarm and regret, in view of the Buddhist precept against taking life, and when he finally went to sleep that night he dreamed that hundreds of frogs came demanding his life.

The monk was terribly upset, but when morning came he looked and found that what he stepped on was an overripe eggplant. At that moment his feeling of uncertainty suddenly stopped, and for the first time he realized the meaning of the saying that "there is no objective world." Then he finally knew how to practice Zen.

8. Moderation

An aged monk, who had lived a long and active life, was assigned a chaplain's role at an academy for girls. In discussion groups he often found that the subject of love became a central topic. This comprised his warning to the young women:

"Understand the danger of anything-too-much in your lives. Too much anger in combat can lead to recklessness and death. Too much ardor in religious beliefs can lead to close-mindedness and persecution.

Too much passion in love creates dream images of the beloved – images that ultimately prove false and generate anger. To love too much is to lick honey from the point of a knife."

"But as a celibate monk," asked one young woman, "how can you know of love between a man and a woman?"

"Sometime, dear children," replied the old teacher, "I will tell you why I became a monk."

9. Buddhism & Christianity

A university student while visiting Gasan asked him: "Have you ever read the Christian Bible?"

"No, read it to me," said Gasan.

The student opened the Bible and read from St. Matthew: "And why take ye thought for rainment? Consider the lilies of the field, how they grow. They toil not, neither do they spin, and yet I say unto you that even Solomon in all his glory was not arrayed like one of these... Take therefore no thought for the morrow, for the morrow shall take thought for the things of itself."

Gasan said: "Whoever uttered those words I consider an enlightened man."

The student continued reading: "Ask and it shall be given you, seek and ye shall find, knock and it shall be opened unto you. For everyone that asketh receiveth, and he that seeketh findeth, and to him that knocketh, it shall be opened."

Gasan remarked: "That is excellent. Whoever said that is not far from Buddhahood."

10. The Hangover

A certain Zen teacher celebrated with his students, drinking sake and whiskey until after midnight, then rose next morning before dawn. Peevish, he expressed annoyance that his American students had not risen in time to do zazen [Zen meditation] before morning service.

When they murmured that their sluggishness might be accounted for by all the drink, the teacher snapped, "Sake is one thing, and zazen is another! They have nothing to do with each other!"

11. God & Air

A hermit was meditating by a river when a young man interrupted him.

"Master, I wish to become your disciple," said the man.

"Why?" replied the hermit.

The young man thought for a moment.

"Because I want to find God."

The master jumped up, grabbed him by the scruff of his neck, dragged him into the river, and plunged his head under water.

After holding him there for a minute, with him kicking and struggling to free himself, the master finally pulled him up out of the river. The young man coughed up water and gasped to get his breath. When he eventually quieted down, the master spoke.

"Tell me, what did you want most of all when you were under water."

"Air!" answered the man.

"Very well," said the master.

"Go home and come back to me when you want God as much as you just wanted air."